Thirty Days to RHYTHM

Ready-to-use Lessons and Reproducible Activities For the Music Classroom

By Betsy Henderson

Table of Contents

ISBN 978-0-634-06586-6

HAL•LEONARD® CORPORATION
7777 W. Bluemound Rd. P.O. Box 13819 Milwaukee, WI 53213

INTRODUCTION / DEFINITION

Name ________________________________

Thirty days has September,
April, June and November.
All our days are filled with rhythm,
Head to toe and inside out.
Days of rhythm, beat and wonder
Make me want to dance and shout!

Adapted

WHAT IS RHYTHM?

We've got rhythm, but what is it exactly? In defining the term **rhythm**, many elements of music are involved.

Rhythm:

- is the organization of musical sounds in time (tempo).
- is measured motion, a grouping of notes based on time value.
- can exist independently, without melody, through speech, body percussion and unpitched instruments.
- is the aspect of music that deals with duration of sound.
- is made up of basic beats and pulses, some more accented and prominent than others.
- is the first essential of melody, giving structure to the upward and downward motion of pitches.

Throughout these thirty lessons on rhythm, apply your natural rhythmical instincts to better understand these concepts:

1. **Beat**
2. **Rhythm of the words** (song text)
3. **Accents** (strong, weak beats)
4. **Duration/Value** (long/short sounds and silences)
5. **Meter** (duple/triple/quadruple)
6. **Syncopation**

Rhythm patterns may be **even, uneven** and/or **syncopated**. Several rhythm components interact in a musical composition; **beat, accent** and the **rhythm of the melody**. In subsequent lessons, you will learn more about these essentials of rhythm.

Learn to correctly spell the word rhythm this way.

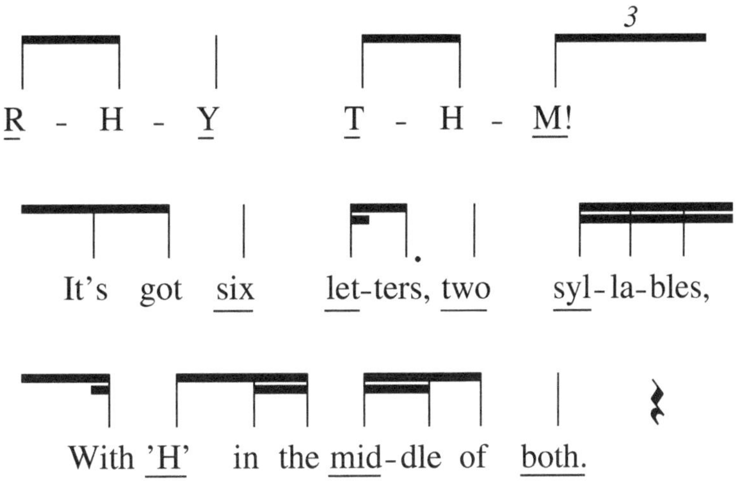

RECOGNIZING RHYTHM

- Have one student read the poem "Thirty Days"(from page 2) aloud randomly.
- After that, have the class read it again together in rhythm, using a steady beat patted lightly on the knees to stay together. Underline the strong beats, then read again with more precision.
- Read the 'spelling of the word rhythm' chant above, using the underlined syllables as the strong beats.
- Play the game "**Rhythm**", with students seated in a circle of numbered chairs, starting with number one through the total number of players. The class keeps this steady beat pattern going: **pat, clap, snap, snap**. As a player's number is called, he must say his own number on the first snap, then another person's number on the second snap. If the rhythm pattern is broken, the player is out, moving to the last chair. All other players move up one chair and renumber so the game can continue. The winner is the person who moves up to chair #1 without breaking the established rhythm.

BONUS QUESTIONS

1. What composer wrote the popular song "I Got Rhythm" in the year 1930?

2. Fill in these blanks with words you learned in this lesson. Rhythm has __________,

   __________, __________ and may have ___________________.

READINESS • 2

VOCABULARY

Name ______________________________

RHYTHM VOCABULARY

As you begin your journey toward being an expert on the subject of rhythm, knowing the proper terminology will assist you in your quest. Follow these suggestions for a more thorough study of important words.

1. Read through the following list of words, placing a check mark by the ones you can already define from previous studies in music theory.
2. Plan a systematic method of learning the remainder of the words (i.e., one a day, one each week, etc.).
3. Make your own personal glossary of terms you will frequently use in projects and assignments, adding other terms as needed.
4. Highlight each of these vocabulary words as they appear in upcoming lessons.
5. Make a set of vocabulary cards to use with a partner in defining the words and using them in sentences.

RHYTHM READINESS VOCABULARY

1. **Accent** – emphasis or stress on a musical tone, beat or chord.
2. ***Alle breve*** – (¢ or cut time) with a time signature of $\frac{2}{2}$.
3. **Bar Line** – a vertical line that divides the staff into measures.
4. **Beat** – the basis unit of time and pulse in music.
5. **Dictation** – the writing of verbal rhythm patterns.
6. **Dot** – added to a note or rest adds one-half the value of that note or rest.
7. **Downbeat** – the first beat of each measure.
8. **Duration** – the length of time value given to specific notes and rests.
9. **Fermata** – a symbol above a note that means to lengthen the note. (𝄐)
10. **Meter** – the regular pattern of beats in a piece of music.
11. **Metronome** – a device for indicating exact tempos.
12. **Notation** – a system of visual symbols for printed music.
13. **Ostinato** – a persistently repeated melodic or rhythmic pattern.
14. **Rondo** – a musical form with repeated theme and contrasting sections. (ABACADA)
15. **Pulse** – a steady, underlying beat.
16. **Syncopation** – the placing of strong accents on usually weak beats.
17. **Tempo** – the pace at which a piece of music is performed.
18. **Triplet** – three notes on one beat. ($\overset{3}{♪♪♪}$)
19. **Rests** – beats of measured silence.
20. **Tie** – a curved line that joins successive notes of the same pitch.

MATCHING TERMS

Put the letter of the word in the right column that best matches the numbered term in the left column.

_____1. steady beat	a. value
_____2. rondo	b. silence
_____3. ostinato	c. device
_____4. duration	d. pattern
_____5. accent	e. hold
_____6. alle breve	f. pulse
_____7. tempo	g. emphasis
_____8. metronome	h. cut time
_____9. rest	i. pace
_____10. fermata	j. ABACADA

After you successfully match the terms, use both words from each matched pair in a written sentence.

SCRAMBLED TERMS

Use your spelling skills to unscramble these terms from the vocabulary list.

1. R O N D I U A T = __ __ __ __ __ __ __ __
2. T A M F R A E = __ __ __ __ __ __ __
3. M O R E E N M T O = __ __ __ __ __ __ __ __ __
4. N T O T I S O A = __ __ __ __ __ __ __ __
5. A O C S N I O T N Y P = __ __ __ __ __ __ __ __ __ __ __

FILL IN THE BLANKS

1. The first beat of each measure is called the ________________________.

2. A dot after a note or rest adds ________________________of that note.

3. Another name for *alle breve* is ________________________.

4. A steady underlying beat is called a ________________________.

5. The purpose of bar lines is to ________________________.

BONUS ACTIVITY

Get ahead by finding the meanings of these terms to be used in upcoming lessons.

1. Anacrusis ________________________

2. Hemiola ________________________

RELEVANCE • 3

STEADY BEAT / PULSE

Name ______________________________

WHAT IS BEAT?

The **beat** is the underlying pulse of the music, which is usually steady with a rate that seldom changes during a musical composition.
Ex. Members of a marching band keep in step with each other because of the music's **steady beat**.

- The steady pulse in music used to measure time is the beat.
- The beat is the most basic element of musical time, forming a background against sounds of varied lengths.
- Like the tick of a clock, beats have a precise, measurable speed or tempo.

STRONG/WEAK

As a younger student, you began to learn how music is organized and structured. You probably practiced tapping, clapping, walking and playing the steady beat.

1. Clap the heartbeats in example #1 above, saying "beat, beat, beat, beat" as you clap.
2. Number the heartbeats from one to four in each box (measure) above, then tap the hearts, counting the numbers aloud as you tap.

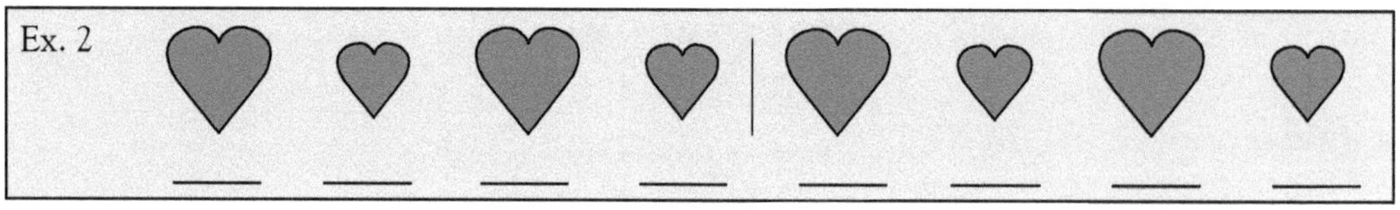

3. Number the heartbeats in example #2 from one to four in each measure. Pat the large heartbeats, saying 'strong' on them and touch your shoulders on the smaller heartbeats as you say 'weak'.

4. Number the heartbeats in example #3 from one to three in each measure, then tap them as you say 'strong – weak – weak'.

GRID ACTIVITIES:

Steady Beat Grid

1	2	3	**4**	**5**	6	7	**8**
1	2	**3**	**4**	5	**6**	7	**8**
1	**2**	3	**4**	**5**	6	7	8
1	**2**	3	4	**5**	6	7	8
1	2	3	**4**	5	6	**7**	8
1	**2**	3	4	**5**	**6**	**7**	8
1	2	**3**	4	5	**6**	7	**8**
1	2	3	4	**5**	6	7	**8**

1. Maintaining a moderate steady beat, read the numbers aloud in this grid, from left to right, one row at a time, clapping as you say the shaded numbers.

2. Repeat the activity, clapping the shaded numbers and snapping the unshaded numbers, counting aloud.

3. Repeat the second step without counting aloud and increase the speed slightly as you go.

4. Divide the class into eight equal groups, assigning each group one specific line to perform. After each group practices, perform all the lines together simultaneously, using clapping and snapping.

5. Repeat step four, giving one person in each group an unpitched instrument to play on the shaded numbers.

6. Perform each line of the grid slowly from top to bottom with a recording of "Canon in D" by Pachebel or a similar piece of music. Perform it again with a faster piece such as "The Stars and Stripes Forever March" by John Philip Sousa.

BONUS QUESTIONS

1. Which number in the grid from top to bottom should sound the loudest when all lines are played simultaneously left to right? Why?

2. Which numbers should sound the softest? Why?

3. Which lines should sound the same? Why?

4. Is it possible to have music with no beat at all? Explain your answer.

5. Two other names for heartbeats in music are ________________ and __________.

RELEVANCE • 4

RHYTHM LANGUAGE

Name ______________________________

RHYTHM SYLLABLES

Students who understand how rhythm works, start by using a special language of **rhythm syllables** to match beats with visual symbols. The basic chart below showing these syllables is based on the **Kodály system of music education** as taught in many American schools. Zoltan Kodály (1882-1967) was a composer and music educator from Hungary who wanted children to build a strong music foundation, starting in their early years.

1. In music with 2, 3 or 4 beats per measure, using a quarter note as one beat, review these rhythm syllables.

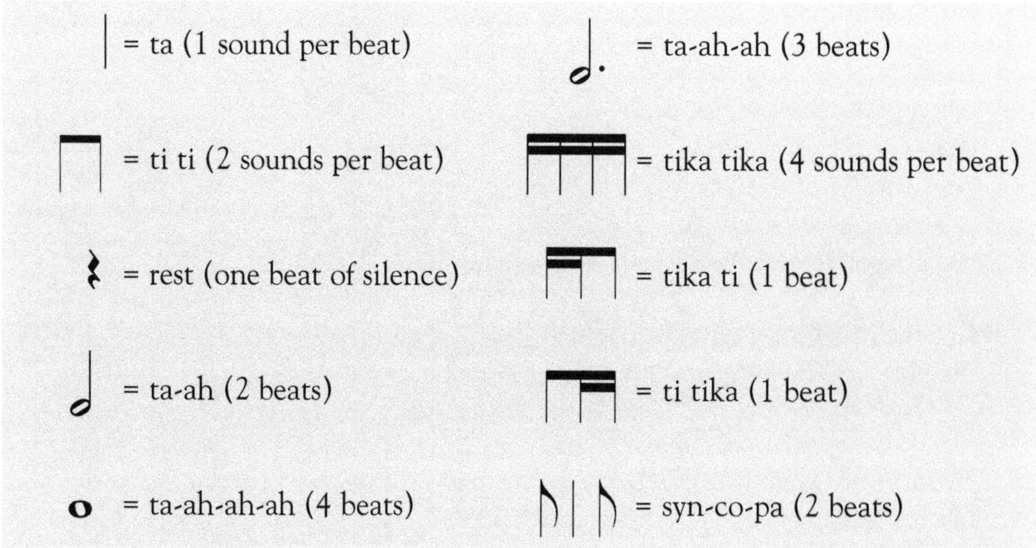

2. In music with 6 beats per measure, using an eighth note as one beat, review these rhythm syllables.

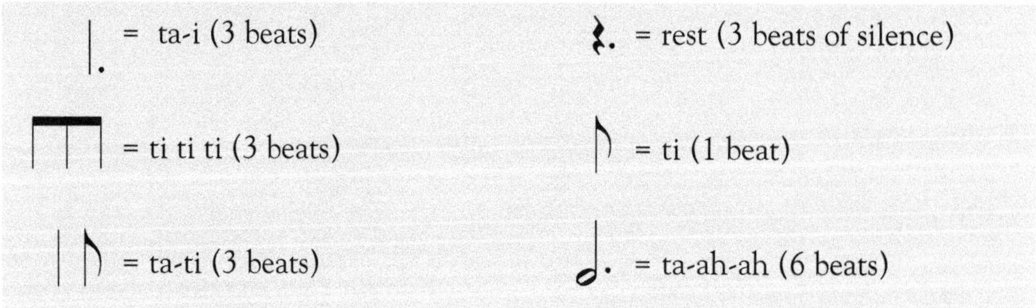

PRACTICE MAKES PERFECT

Tap this line, saying the rhythm syllables **ta** (|), **ti** (♪) or **ti ti** (⊓) aloud. (3 beats per measure)

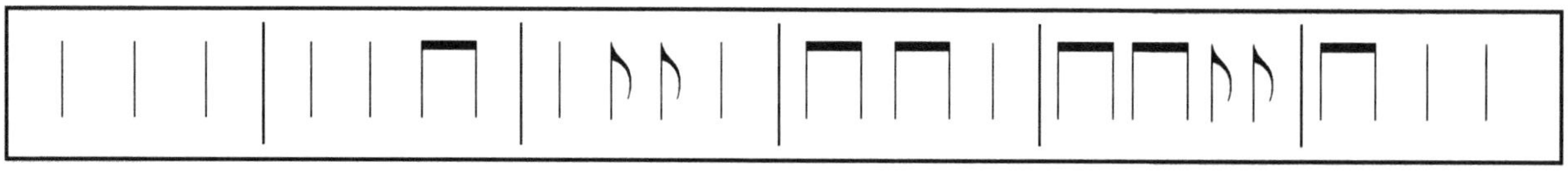

Clap each line, saying the rhythm syllables **ta** (|), **ti** (♪) or **ti ti** (⊓) aloud. (4 beats per measure)

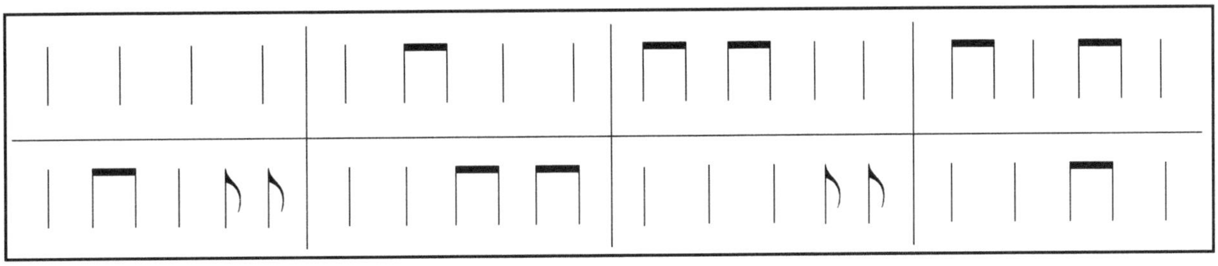

Pat this line, saying the added rhythm syllables **ta-ah** (𝅗𝅥) and **rest** (𝄽) with the others.

RHYTHM BINGO

- Provide the game board below on paper, a transparency or chalkboard.
- Divide the class into two equal, alternating teams.
- Each player selects a box to perform, clapping the rhythm and saying the syllables.
- If done correctly, the box is covered with a token chosen by that team (paper square, circle, flag or star, etc.)
- The team who gets a full line of tokens wins the game.

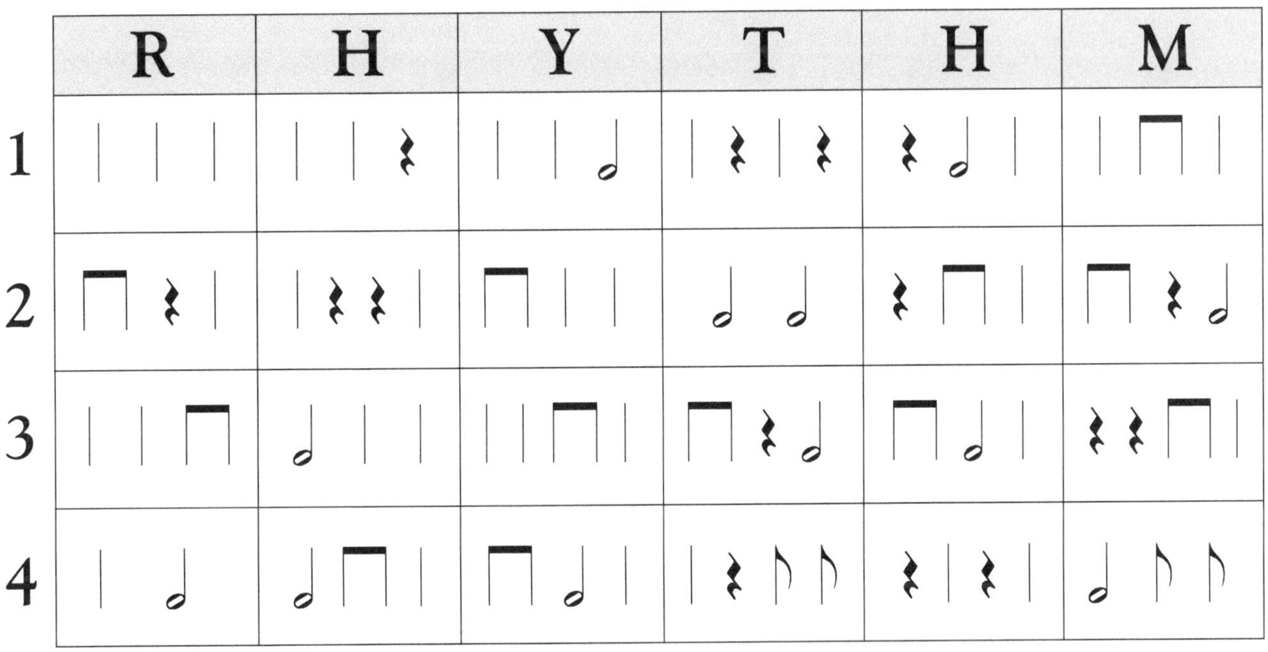

RELEVANCE • 5

RHYTHM OF THE WORDS

Name ______________________________

RHYTHM OF THE WORDS

Over the steady, underlying beat, music moves in sounds that are longer, shorter, the same or silent. Without any melody or lyric, the rhythm structure of a familiar song looks like this:

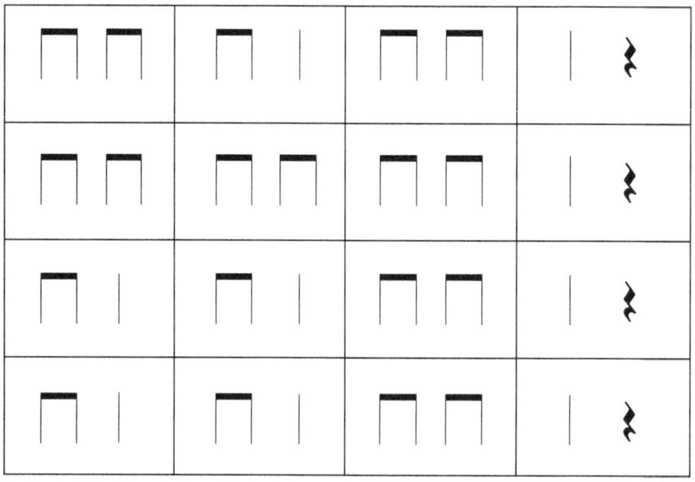

- Tap and say the rhythm syllables for each line separately, then try the whole song all the way through with a steady beat.
- Find the lines that are exactly alike rhythmically.
- Now tap the **rhythm of the words** to this same American folk song, "Old Joe Clarke."

"Old Joe Clarke, he had a house, sixteen stories high;
Ev'ry story in that house was filled with chicken pie.
Round and round, old Joe Clarke, round and round I say,
Round and round, old Joe Clarke, ain't got long to stay."

Say the **rhythm syllables** to the right of another familiar folk song, as you pat a steady beat.

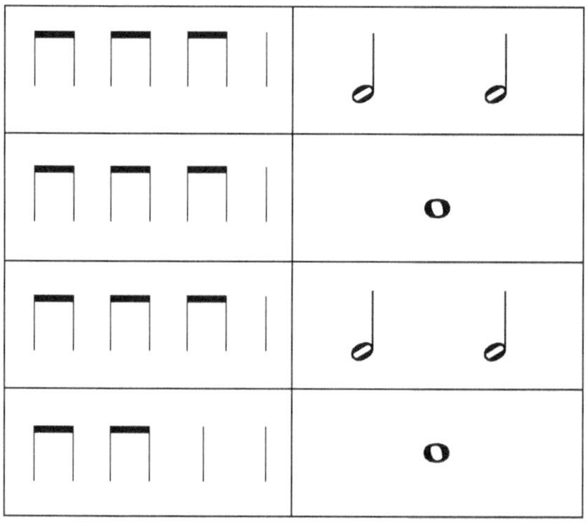

Did you recognize the rhythm of the folksong, "Dinah"?

Someone's in the kitchen with Dinah,
Someone's in the kitchen, I know ———.
Someone's in the kitchen with Dinah,
Strummin' on the old banjo———.

- Choose and face a partner, with palms up toward each other.
- One student will pat a steady beat with right hand on the partner's left hand.
- The other partner will tap the 'word rhythm' of the song above, using the right hand on the partner's left.
- Both parts start at the same time as the words to "Dinah" are said aloud by both partners.
- When successful, switch parts and repeat the activity.

RHYTHM OF THE NAME

Rhythm syllables can help us sound out our names and write them down using rhythm language.

Ex. Robert Foster: [| | | |]	Emily Brown: [ ]	Teddy McPherson: [ ]
Dulciana York: [ ]	Bob Jones: [ ]	Amber Williams: [ ]

- In the boxes above these names, write the corresponding rhythm syllables.
- Figure out your own name using rhythm syllables, asking a partner for help as needed. [ ]
- Create an eight-beat rhythm pattern using names of people in your class. Write it out and share it with the group.

MATCH RHYTHM WITH WORDS

_____1. Africa	a. | |
_____2. England	b. | ⊓ |
_____3. Central America	c. ⊓ |
_____4. United States	d. ♪ | |
_____5. Alaska	e. | ⊓ ⊓ |

BONUS QUESTION

What is the form of "Old Joe Clarke"? ____________

MAKING NOTES / NOTATION

Name ______________________________

MAKING NOTES

Now that you have used rhythm syllables and symbols, it is time to utilize regular notation in the reading of rhythm. Notating rhythm involves the following symbols:

- a **notehead** that is placed on a line or space of the staff.
- a **stem** for all notes except the whole note.
- **flags** that join the stem at the opposite end from the notehead.
- **beams** are often used instead of flags to join similar notes together.

Noteheads can be filled in or left open, depending on the value of the note. **Stems** can point either up or down, depending on the placement on a staff. If stems are on notes placed above the third line of the staff, they go on the left side, extending downward. If the note is below the third line, the stem is on the right side, extending upward. Stems on notes placed on the third line may extend either way. Stems are made long enough to pass through three lines or three spaces on the staff, wherever placed.

From one to five **flags** indicate change in the value of the note; the more flags, the shorter the sound. Flags pass through two spaces or lines of the staff. The flag is always on the right side of the note stem, extending upward if the stem does down and downward if the stem goes up.

Label the parts of the notes in the examples above on the lines provided.

Below are the most commonly used notes. Each note in succession represents a duration length half as long as the note that precedes it in this order.

WHOLE HALF QUARTER EIGHTH SIXTEENTH

Practice making several of each of these commonly used notes in the boxes below.

In this example, notes are placed on a music staff. Putting notes on a staff is a precise task because the accuracy of the melodic line depends on it.

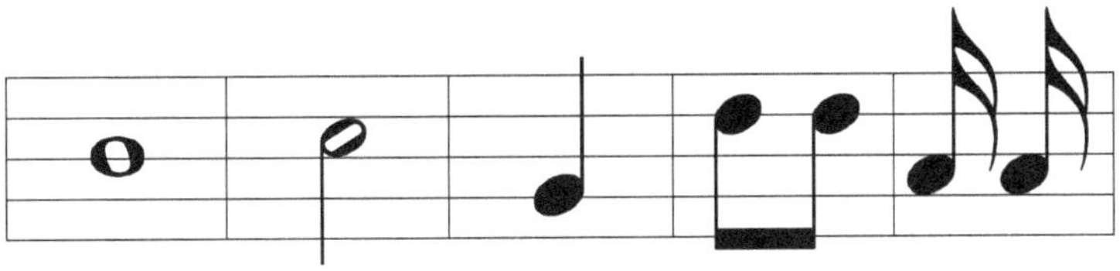

Practice making several of each commonly used notes on the staff below.

MAKE A MUSIC MOSAIC

Draw a circle around all quarter notes, a square around all eighth notes, a triangle around all half notes, and a diamond around all whole notes. Using markers, colored pencils or crayons, add some color to your mosaic design.

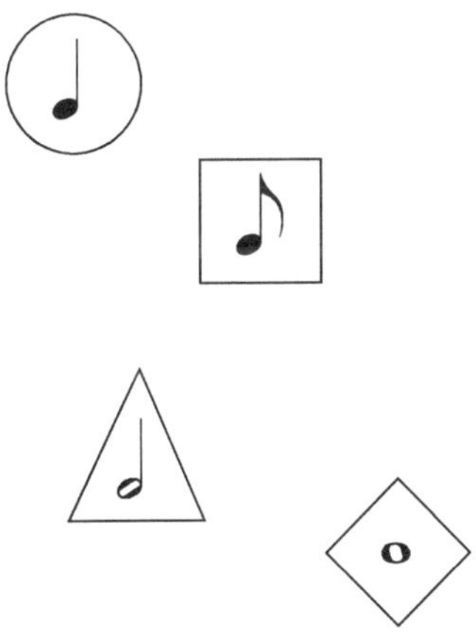

BONUS QUESTIONS

1. What would a note with three flags be called? ______________________________

2. How do you join four sixteenth notes together? ______________________________

3. Which notes never have flags or beams? ______________________________

NOTE VALUES / DURATION

Name ______________________________

NOTE VALUES

The shape of the note is the clue to its duration. The most commonly used note values are the **whole note**, **half note**, **quarter note**, **eighth note** and the **sixteenth note**. In this order, each one lasts half as long as the previous mentioned note, as pictured below:

As shown in 'hierarchy' order, this chart displays how each note relates to the others. Notice that the whole note is on top with each level below the whole note representing a value that is one-half the value of the note above it. In other words, since a half note gets half the value of a whole note, it takes two of them to fill the same measure.

Whole note

Half notes

Quarter notes

Eighth notes

Sixteenth notes

CLUES

Fill in the blanks below each box with the name of the correct note and its beat value in $\frac{4}{4}$ meter based on the clue, then write the note inside the box provided.

Clue: Has two flags or beams	**Clue:** Has one flag or beam	**Clue:** Has a stem but not filled in	**Clue:** Has no stem or flag	**Clue:** Has a stem, is filled in but no flag

Note Name:

_______________ _______________ _______________ _______________ _______________

Beat Value:

_______________ _______________ _______________ _______________ _______________

MUSIC AND MATH

Another way to understand how one note relates to the others is to see the similarities between note values and fractions.

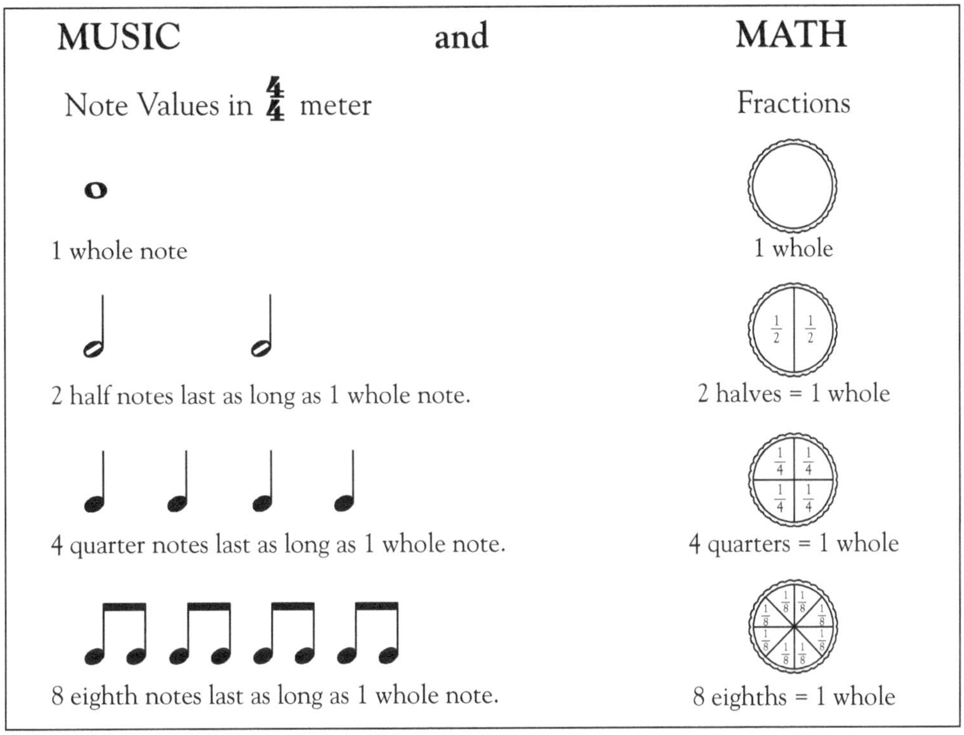

DOES IT ADD UP?

Use your math skills by putting **T (true)** in the blank if the beats are equal in value or **F (false)** if they are not. Tell a partner why specific examples are false.

______ 1. 𝅝 = ♩ ♩ ♫ ♩

______ 2. 𝅗𝅥 𝅗𝅥 = ♫ ♫ ♩

______ 3. ♪ ♪ ♩ ♩ = ♫ ♫

______ 4. ♩ ♩ = 𝅗𝅥

______ 5. 𝅗𝅥 ♫ ♩ = 𝅝

Write notes to fill these boxes with the designated number of beats, none alike; then clap the rhythms as you say the rhythm patterns you created.

Two Beats	**Two Beats**	**Three Beats**	**Three Beats**	**Four Beats**	**Four Beats**

BONUS QUESTIONS

1. How many sixteenth notes would equal three whole notes?________________

2. Figure out the number of total beats from this equation: ________________

𝅝 + 𝅗𝅥 − ♩ + ♫ × 𝅝 + 𝅗𝅥 = ___?___

RESTS / BEATS OF SILENCE

Name ______________________________

For each note introduced in the previous lesson, there is also a **rest** that is named the same and is given the same number of (silent) beats as the corresponding note. When reading rhythm patterns or phrases, these beats of silence must be counted. Time doesn't stop in music, even when no sound is heard.

DURATION OF NOTE AND REST VALUES

The length of time assigned to a note or a rest is indicated so the performer will know how long to play or sing each note or how long to be silent.

NOTES	RESTS	BEATS
𝅝 Whole note	𝄻 Whole rest	4 beats
𝅗𝅥 Half note	𝄼 half rest	2 beats
♩ Quarter note	𝄽 quarter rest	1 beat
♪ Eighth note	𝄾 eighth rest	½ beat
𝅘𝅥𝅯 Sixteenth note	𝄿 sixteenth rest	¼ beat

MATCH THEM UP

Put a letter in each blank to match the correct note with the corresponding rest.

__________1. 𝅘𝅥𝅯 a. 𝄼
__________2. 𝅝 b. 𝄽
__________3. ♩ c 𝄾
__________4. 𝅗𝅥 d. 𝄻
__________5. ♪ e. 𝄿

When placing rests on a staff, notice that the **half rest** sits on the third line of the staff and a **whole rest** hangs down from the fourth line. All other rests are centered.

Half Rest

Whole Rest

Practice making each rest, first in a box, then on a staff correctly.

Whole Rest	Half Rest	Quarter Rest	Eighth Rest	Sixteenth Rest

USING THE RESTS

Say these rhythm syllables below with a steady beat, then tap them as you repeat each line. Say 'rest' on the rests, and put hands out with palms up to designate the silent beats.

1.
2.
3.

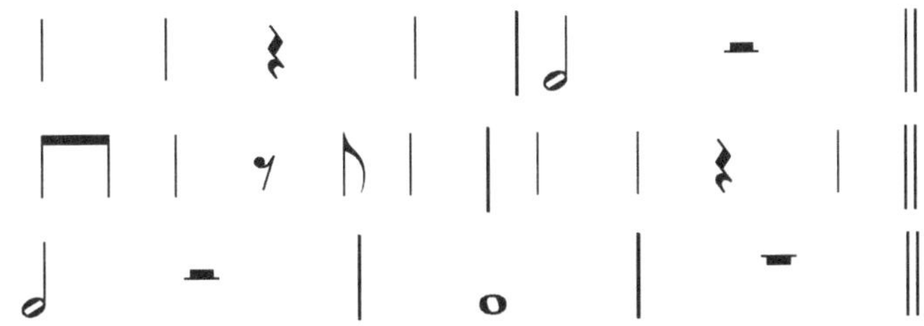

MUSIC AND MATH TEAM UP

Use your math and music skills to fill in the blanks.

1. 𝄽 is to ♩ as 𝄼 is to ________.
2. 𝄾 is to ♪ as ________ is to ♩ .
3. 𝄼 is to 𝅗𝅥 as 𝅝 is to ________.
4. 𝄿 is to 𝅘𝅥𝅯 as ________ is to ♩ .
5. 𝄼 is to 𝄻 as 𝄾 is to ________.
6. ♪ is to 𝅘𝅥𝅯 as ________ is to 𝅗𝅥 .

BONUS QUESTIONS

1. Is it possible for a rest to have three flags? What would it be called and what would be its beat value?

2. How many total beats in 4 beat meter would these rests equal? ________________

(𝄻 𝄻) – (𝄾 + 𝄾) + (𝄼 + 𝄼) – (𝄽 + 𝄽) = ?

MEASURES / BAR LINES

Name ______________________________

MEASURES / BAR LINES

Music is divided into **measures**, which are groupings of beats separated by vertical lines through the staff called **bar lines**.

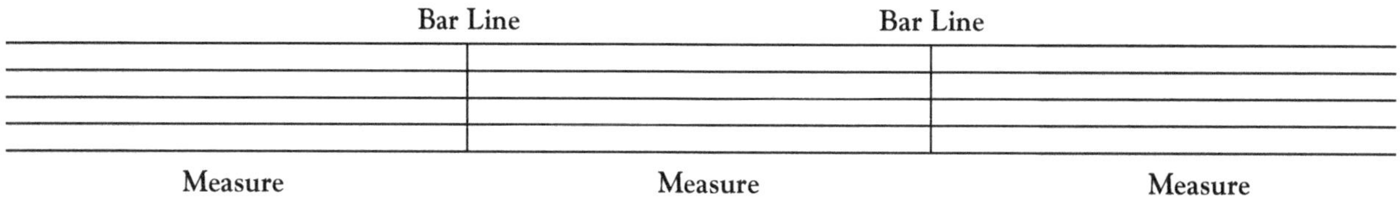

The bar line, as we know it today, did not exist before the 17th Century. With no bar lines, the music had more relaxed flow to it than strict meter, making individual melodic and harmonic lines hard to follow.

Usually the first beat of each measure is given more emphasis than the other bests, and is performed with an accent. Clap and count these beats, stressing the first beat of each measure.

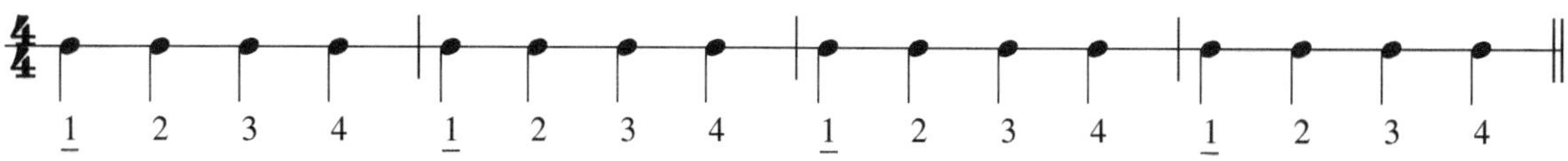

4 = 4 beats per measure
4 =quarter note gets one beat

(A detailed study of Time Signatures comes in Lesson 12.)

The **double bar line**, consisting of a thin, vertical line followed by a darker line, is found at the end of a piece of music, signifying that the composition is finished. If **two dots are added**, this is an indication to repeat a section or all of the song.

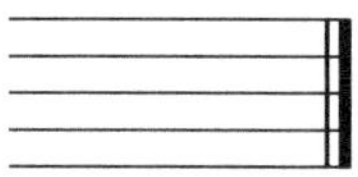

Double Bar Line

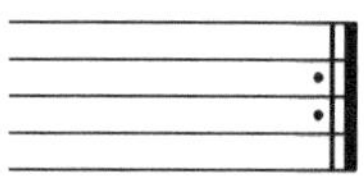

Repeat Sign

Add bar lines to the following examples:

COUNTING THE RHYTHM

When **two equal sounds are shown on one beat** ( ), clap and count them by saying the number of the beat on the first note, then add "and" on the second note.

Ex. 

When clapping **half notes**, clap and say the number on the first beat, then keep hands clasped as you say the second beat. Another method is to tap the first beat in the palm, then slide the fingers over the hand for the second beat.

Ex. 

For a **whole note**, extend the method above two beats longer.

Ex. 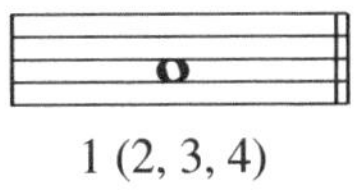

Study each line below, counting the beats, then circle the measures that do not have the correct number of counts.

1. 

2. 

3. 

BONUS QUESTION

Write in the counts under this example, then practice counting and clapping it.

RHYTHM RECAP / TEST YOUR KNOWLEDGE

Name ____

In the first nine lessons, you have had the opportunity to learn important information about **steady beat**, **rhythm syllables**, **notes**, **rests** and **counting rhythm**. Use this review to see how much you remember and can utilize in understanding how rhythm works in music.

1. Give your own definition of these terms.

   a. *Duration* ______________________________

   b. *Accent* ______________________________

2. Write four measures of 'heartbeats', one heart for each beat, separating the measures with bar lines. Clap them as you say '**ta**' on each one. Next, clap the beats again, emphasizing the first beat each time.

3. Study the example below using three beats per measure and draw in a rest (𝄽) where a beat is missing, then read the rhythm syllables of the line.

4. Write your own measures in these empty boxes using four beats in each one, making your measures different from the example provided. Clap what you write, saying '**ta**', '**ti**' and '**rest**' as appropriate.

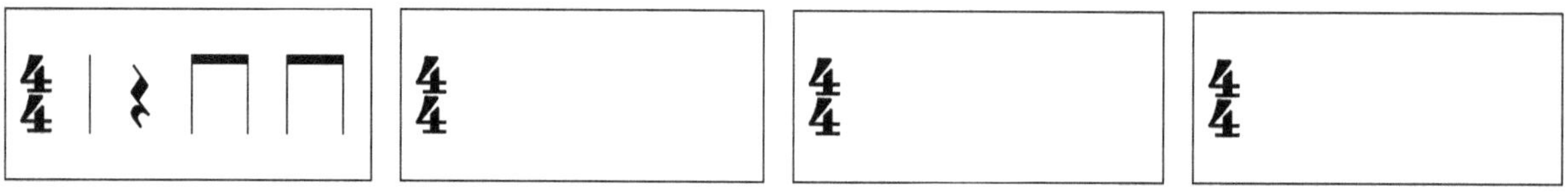

5. Make several notes below as instructed.

Quarter Note	Sixteenth Note	Half Note	Eighth Note	Whole Note

6. Name the three parts of notes.

____

____

____

7. Say the words of the chorus of the folk song, "Bingo" (*B-i-ngo, B-i-ngo, B-i-ngo, and Bingo was his name-o*) as you tap a steady beat. Finish the rhythm symbols for the chorus below, putting one "Bingo" in each box. Where will the word "and" go?

B I N G O | | ⊓ |			

8. Underline the stressed beats in the line you wrote above.

9. Fill in the blanks.

- Which rest has the same value as 𝅗𝅥 ? ____________
- Which note has the same value as ▬ ? ____________
- ____________ half notes equal one whole note.
- A half note equals ____________ eighth notes.
- Four quarter notes equal a ____________.
- ____________ quarter notes equal ⊓ ⊓ .
- A ▬ and a ____________ note have the same value.
- Add ____________ to a half note to equal a whole note.

10. True or False: If the sets of notes/rests equal the same number of beats, put "T" in the blank, or put "F" if not.

a. _____ ♩ ♩ = ▬

b. _____ ♪ ♩ ♪ = 𝄿 𝄿

c. _____ ⊓ ⊓ = 𝄽 𝄽

d. _____ 𝅝 = ▬

e. _____ 𝅗𝅥 𝅗𝅥 = ▬

f. _____ ♩ ♩ ♩ = 𝄾 𝄾 𝄾

g. _____ ⊓ | ⊓ | = ▬

h. _____ ⊓ = 𝄽

11. Count the Beats: Count the beats in each example and put the number in the blank:

a. _____ ♫ ♫ ♩

b. _____ ♫ 𝅗𝅥 ♩

c. _____ 𝅝

d. _____ 𝅗𝅥 𝄽 ♩

FLASHCARDS / PRACTICE AND GAMES

Name ______________________________

When you were learning the multiplication facts in math class, flashcards made that task easier and more fun. You are encouraged to make a small set of **rhythm flashcards** (3 X 5) for your personal use and have one large class set of cards (8½ X 11) made for games and competition.

LEVEL ONE

Suggestions For Using Flashcard Sets One and Two:

1. Practice clapping the patterns on your own, as you say the rhythm syllables.
2. Work with a partner as you challenge each other and keep points.
3. Have a leader hold up one card at a time for the class to repeat.
4. Divide into teams within the class for a "rhythm bee" to establish a winning team.
5. Put several cards together to create longer rhythm patterns to read and clap.

Flashcards: SET ONE

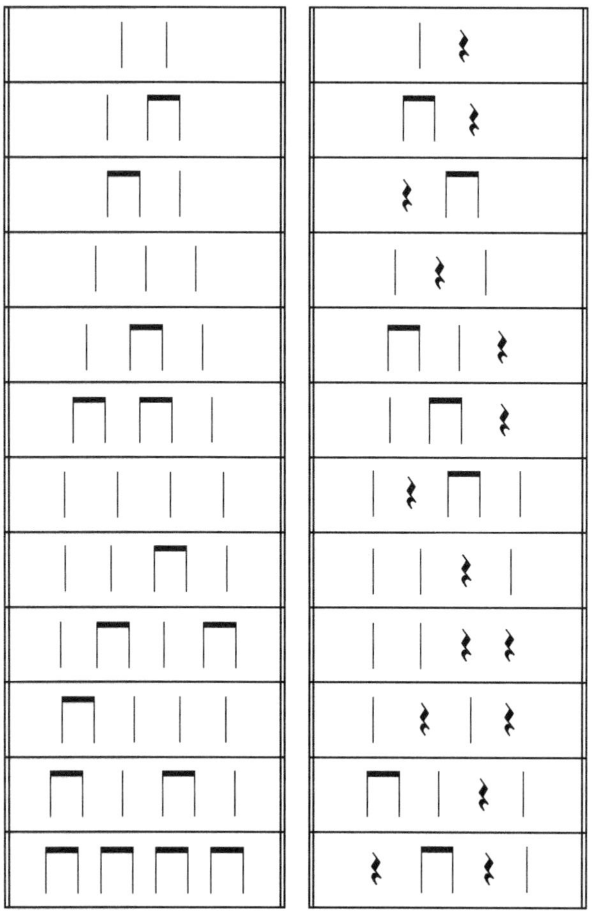

Flashcards: SET TWO

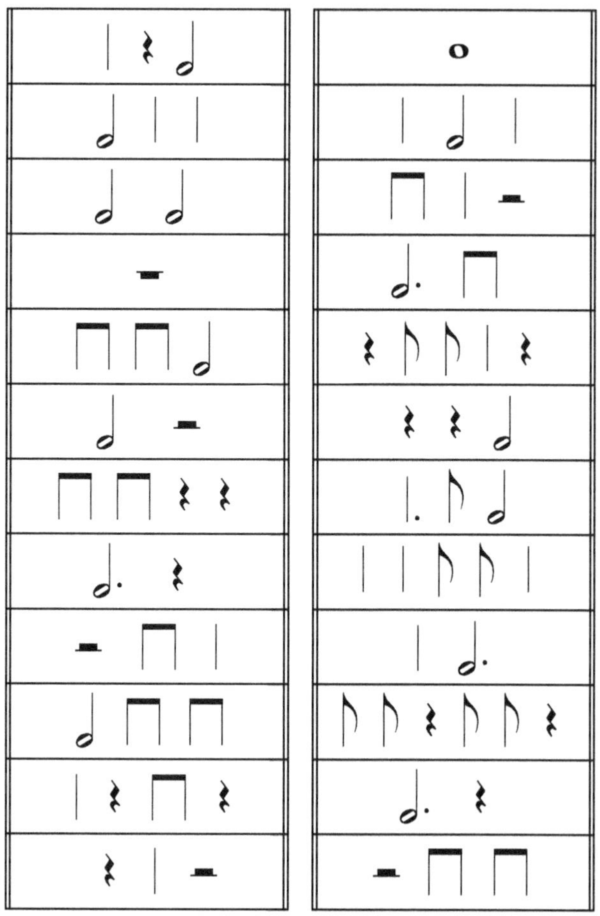

LEVEL TWO

Suggestions for Using Flashcard Sets Three and Four:

1. Put several measures together in certain time signatures to comprise phrases of songs.
2. Use the cards in this sequence: read syllables, read and count aloud, read and clap, clap only, then play the pattern on an unpitched instrument.
3. Set up cards for eight measures and perform as a canon in two groups, the second group starting one measure after the first group begins.
4. Read/clap cards in a continuous pace as the leader shows each card in rapid motion.
5. Find rhythm patterns from the cards that match names of students in your class.

Flashcards: SET THREE

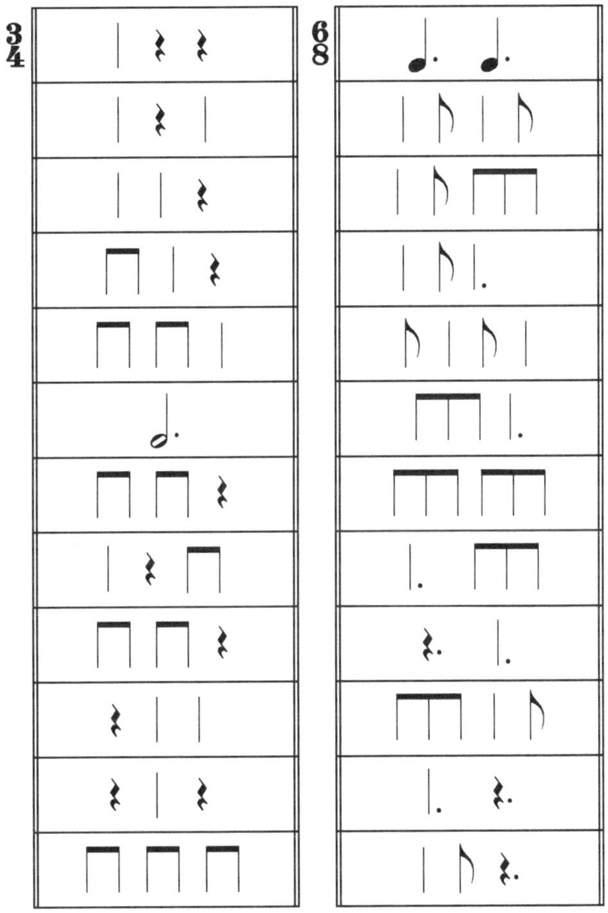

Flashcards: SET FOUR

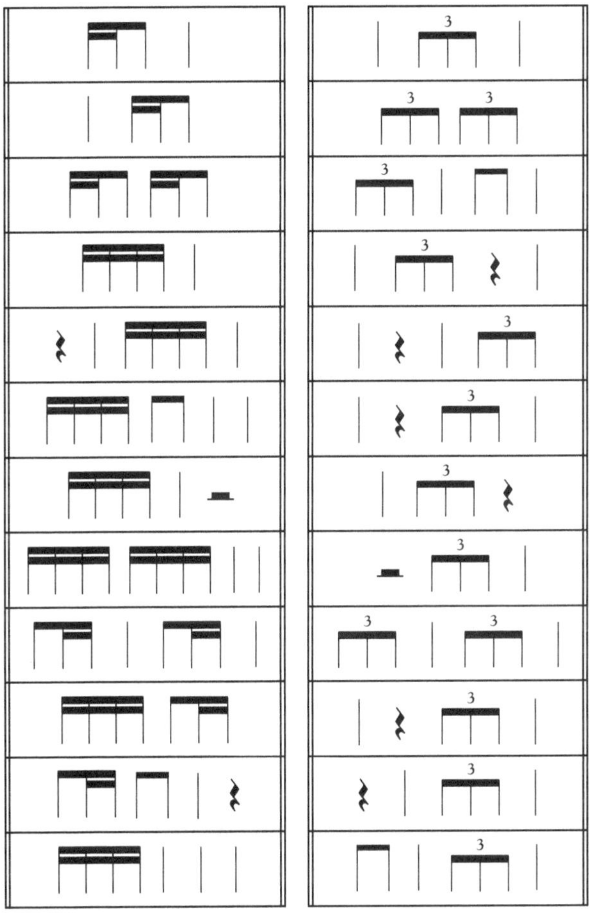

BONUS QUESTIONS

1. Can you find and isolate patterns from the flashcards in printed song material?

2. Can you make word phrases to fit rhythm patterns on selected flashcards?

TIME SIGNATURES

Name ______________________________

WHAT IS A TIME SIGNATURE?

The **meter (or time) signature** is found at the beginning of the staff, following the clef sign and key signature (sharps or flats). It consists of two numbers, one on top of the other.

Ex. 

The **top number** indicates how many beats are in each measure and the **bottom number** tells what kind of note gets one beat (half note = 2 on the bottom, quarter note = 4 on the bottom and eighth note = 8 on the bottom).

Ex.			
3	= three beats in each measure	**6**	= six beats in each measure
4	= a quarter note gets one beat	**8**	= an eighth note gets one beat

The top number is usually between one and twelve, but the numbers two, four and eight are the most common bottom numbers. It is not necessary to show the time signature on each line of music after it is once indicated, unless the meter changes within the piece. A time signature is not written as a fraction with a dividing mark between the numbers.

The most frequently used time signatures are listed below. *(These meters will be discussed in Lesson 13.)*

- duple meter $\genfrac{}{}{0pt}{}{2}{2}$ $\genfrac{}{}{0pt}{}{2}{4}$ $\genfrac{}{}{0pt}{}{2}{8}$
- triple meter $\genfrac{}{}{0pt}{}{3}{2}$ $\genfrac{}{}{0pt}{}{3}{4}$ $\genfrac{}{}{0pt}{}{3}{8}$ $\genfrac{}{}{0pt}{}{3}{16}$
- quadruple meter $\genfrac{}{}{0pt}{}{4}{4}$ $\genfrac{}{}{0pt}{}{4}{8}$

APPLY WHAT YOU KNOW

Describe what these numbers mean in various meters.

6 = ______________________________
8 = ______________________________

3 = ______________________________
4 = ______________________________

3 = ______________________________
2 = ______________________________

Fill in the time signatures for these examples.

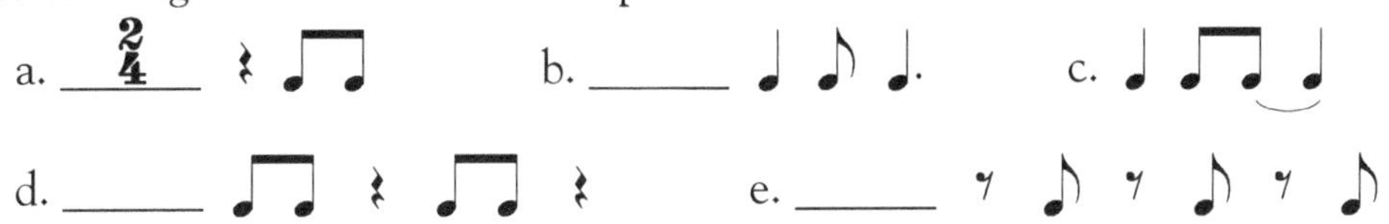

A SIMPLER SYMBOL

Sometimes in music, a simpler symbol for the time signature may be shown, as a number on top with the specified note underneath. This is a more graphic usage found often in textbooks and printed music.

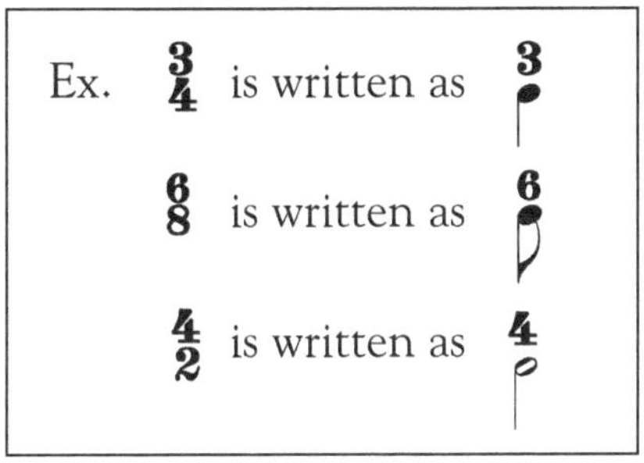

SHORT CUTS

Two other time signature symbols are often used instead of numbers. The first of these 'short-cut' symbols is a capital 'C' centered on the staff, used for pieces in $\frac{4}{4}$ time, often called **common time**. The other refers to **cut time** (*alle breve*), used for pieces in $\frac{2}{2}$ time, made like a capital 'C' with a vertical line drawn through it. It means to give each note one-half of its defined value. These time signatures are actually leftover symbols from the late 13th century to the late 16th century, then called mensural notation.

Ex.

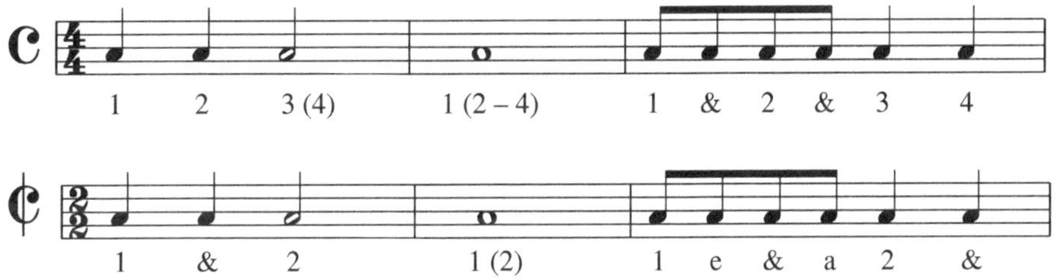

MORE PRACTICE

Practice these rhythm patterns in simple time by marking the strong beats, counting and clapping each pattern several times.

13

SIMPLE METER

Name ______________________________

METER

Rhythm and meter are slightly different aspects of music, but closely related. Where rhythm refers to note values and duration, **meter** refers to the basic underlying beat of strong and weak pulses.

The term meter also corresponds to time signatures, the important numbers found at the beginning of a piece of music for counting purposes. Meter is the fundamental structure of time on which rhythm and tempo are placed.

Three types of meter are *duple* (two beats per measure), *triple* (three beats per measure) and *quadruple* (four beats per measure).

Ex. **Simple - Duple Meter**

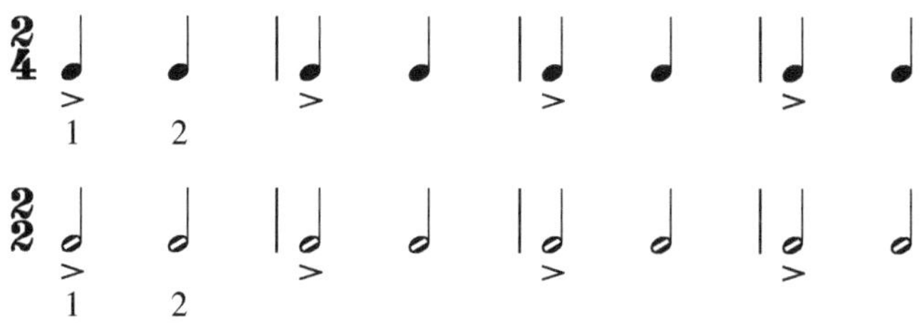

Simple - Triple Meter

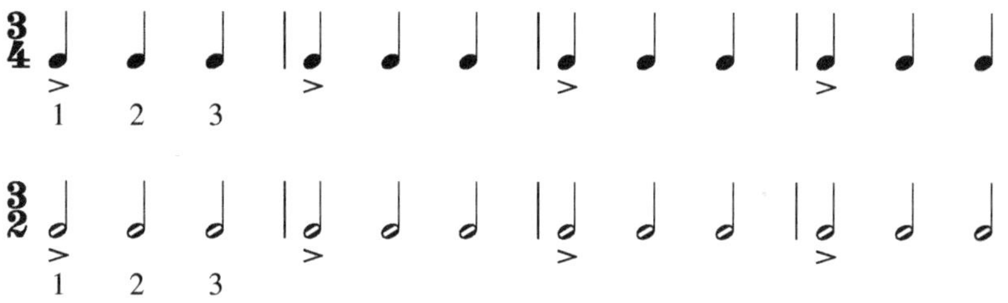

Simple - Quadruple Meter

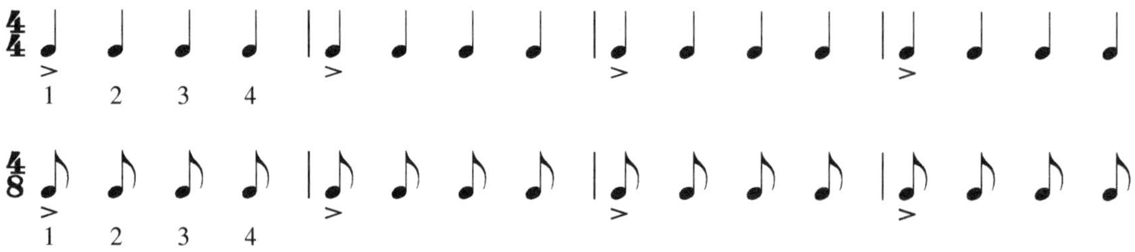

Practice clapping the examples above in duple, triple and quadruple meters, observing the strong beats marked by ">".

EXPERIMENTING WITH METERS

Duple meter contains two beats to each measure, with the accent falling on the first beat. For example, try singing the song, "Yankee Doodle," as you pat a 'strong-weak, strong-weak' pattern with a steady beat.

Triple meter has three beats per measure, accenting the first beat. Music including waltzes, jazz waltzes and minuets are performed in triple meter. Practice singing "My Country 'Tis of Thee" as you pat a 'strong-weak-weak, strong-weak-weak' pattern with a steady underlying beat.

Another name for **quadruple meter** is Common Time, containing four beats per measure. A strong accent falls on the first beat of each measure, with a secondary accent on the third beat. Use the "Battle Hymn of the Republic" as an example to help you sing a song in quadruple meter, patting a 'strong-weak-weak-weak, strong-weak-weak-weak' pattern.

Listen to some your favorite music to discover the meter. Particularly listen for the strong and weak beats within each measure. Many of the most widely sung songs are sung in 'Common Time' with four beats per measure (quadruple meter), including country, jazz, gospel, folk and rock music.

QUESTIONS/PRACTICE

1. Write the words, 'strong and weak' to indicate beat patterns for duple and triple meter.

Duple ____________________ **Triple** ____________________

2. In quadruple meter, the ________ and ________beats are strong and the ________and ________beats are weak, with the ______________ beat being the strongest.

3. A 'strong-weak-weak' pattern is know as __________________meter.

4. In this example, put (S) under the strong beats and (W) under the weak ones.

LISTENING EXAMPLES

Locate and listen to these examples of various meters, patting the strong and weak beats as you enjoy the music:

1. **Duple** – *"Overture No. 2 in B minor, Badinerie"* by J.S. Bach
2. **Triple** – *"On the Beautiful, Blue Danube"* by Johann Strauss II
3. **Quadruple** – *"Hallelujah Chorus"* from the MESSIAH by G. F. Handel

COMPOUND METER

Name ______________________________

COMPOUND METER

Compound meters are simple meters with a top number that has been multiplied by three, such as 6/4 and 6/8. The most common compound meters are shown below.

Ex.

𝅗𝅥. = basic beat

6/4 (2/𝅗𝅥.)   9/4 (3/𝅗𝅥.)   12/4 (4/𝅗𝅥.)

♪ = basic beat

6/16 (2/♪.)   9/16 (3/♪.)   12/16 (4/♪.)

♩. = basic beat

6/8 (2/♩.)   9/8 (3/♩.)   12/8 (4/♩.)

The most common compound meter is 6/8 which means there will be six beats per measure and an eighth note gets one beat.

Ex. **6** = 6 counts per measure
8 = eighth (♪) note receives one count

Songs written in 6/8 meter can be performed in two ways. One way is to count six equal beats per measure, but in the second way, two strong beats per measure (on 1 and 4) are felt with a dotted quarter note getting one beat.

Ex. 1   1 2 3 4 5 6   Ex. 2   <u>1</u> 2 3 <u>4</u> 5 6

MATH AND METER

Make note of this chart showing the basic notes and their values in 6/8 meter below. Make use of your math and music skills to fill in the blank boxes in the chart below.

NOTES	Eighth Note ♪	Quarter Note ♩	Three Eighth Notes ♫♪	Dotted Quarter Note ♩.	Dotted Half Note 𝅗𝅥.
COUNTS	1	2	3	3	6

TIME SIGNATURE	6/8	6/4	9/16	9/8	12/8	12/4
BEATS PER MEASURE	2		3		4	
BASIC BEAT NOTE		𝅗𝅥.		♩.		𝅗𝅥.

Underline two strong beats per measure in this example, then clap it several times.

Sing "Row, Row, Row Your Boat" (two times) or "Take Me Out to the Ball Game" (four times) as you clap the $\frac{6}{8}$ pattern.

COMPARE SIMPLE & COMPOUND

Just like simple meters, compound meters are called duple, triple and quadruple meters, depending on the number of basic beats in each measure.

Ex.				
	Compound – duple	$\frac{6}{4}$	$\frac{6}{2}$	$\frac{6}{8}$
	Compound – triple	$\frac{9}{4}$	$\frac{9}{8}$	
	Compound – quadruple	$\frac{12}{4}$	$\frac{12}{8}$	

Finish writing in the rhythm syllables for this poem; the first in simple meter and the second in compound meter. Practice saying the poem aloud both ways as you clap the rhythm.

BONUS ACTIVITIES

1. Divide the class in half, each group clapping one line of the example below at the same time, then switch parts and repeat.
2. In small groups, create your own words to fit the rhythm below, then share with the group.

RESOURCES • 14

15

IRREGULAR METER

Name ______________________________

There are accepted exceptions to the established standards of meter introduced in the previous lesson. Do some research about the following exceptions to the rules to find out more interesting information:

EXCEPTIONS TO THE RULES

- **Nonmetric** – Music with no steady beat, no time signature and no defined measures is considered nonmetric.
- **Complex** – Imperfect or assymetrical music is called complex, including meters made up of mixed simple meters. Meters of five, seven beats and larger which can only be divided unequally were rarely used before the 20th century.

Ex. $\frac{3}{2}$ $\frac{5}{4}$ $\frac{7}{4}$ $\frac{9}{4}$ $\frac{5}{8}$ $\frac{7}{8}$

$\frac{5}{4}$ meter indicates five beats in each measure with a quarter note getting one beat. Notice that $\frac{5}{4}$ meter can be divided into 2 beats + 3 beats or 3 beats + 2 beats, depending on where the stressed beats fall.

Ex.

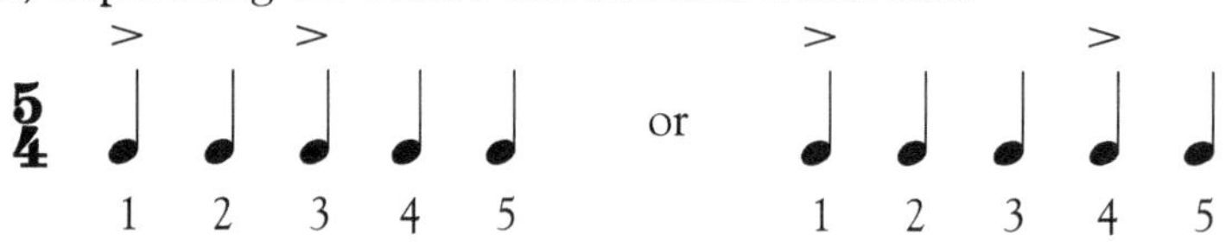

Practice clapping these $\frac{5}{4}$ examples as you count aloud.

- **Quintuple** – Music with five beats per measure is also called quintuple meter with two strong beats present in each measure. Instead of an 'oom-pa-pa, oom-pa-pa' pattern with six beats per measures, one would hear 'oom-pa, oom-pa-pa' instead, using five beats.

To hear an example of complex (quintuple) meter, locate and listen to 'Mars' from Holst's "*Planets*" (3 + 2 beats in each measure). A dramatic quintuple rhythm gives this piece a foreboding sound.

- **Multimeter** indicates the use of numerous time signature changes in very quick succession within a piece of music (i. e. two measures of $\frac{3}{4}$, followed by one measure of $\frac{2}{4}$, followed by three measures of $\frac{3}{8}$, etc.)
- **Polyrhythms** are two contrasting rhythms, perhaps in different meters, played or sung at the same time. As a result, the stressed beats often come at different and conflicting times.

To experience 'polyrhythms', have half of the class sing "My Country 'Tis of Thee" (three beats per measure) as the other half sings "America, the Beautiful" (four beats per measure) **at the same time.**

Ex.

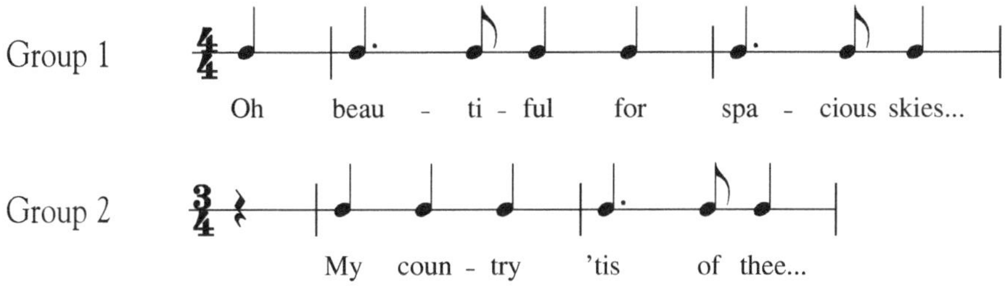

- A **hemiola** depends on the fact that six beats can be divided into two groups of three beats or three groups of two beats. In Leonard Bernstein's popular musical *"West Side Story"*, an example of the hemiola is heard in the song, "America" and also in some Spanish music. The effect is a sense of slowing down without actually changing the tempo.

Ex. ||: 1̂ 2 3 1̂ 2 3 | 1̂ 2 1̂ 2 1̂ 2 :||

Practice clapping and counting these examples.

- A **cross-rhythm**, just as in polyrhythm, happens when two conflicting rhythms are heard at the same time. The composer, Chopin, in *"Waltz in A flat", opus 42*, wrote the melody in duple time for the right hand, but developed a 'strong-weak-weak' waltz rhythm for the left hand at the same time. Seldom heard in Western music, cross rhythms are found often in African music.

- When a group of three notes is written in the time usually filled by two notes, the pattern is called a **triplet**. Most commonly found in eighth notes, triplets can also be formed by quarter and half notes. You can recognize a triplet pattern by a number 3 above it.

Ex.

Circle the triplets below, then clap and count these examples using triplet patterns.

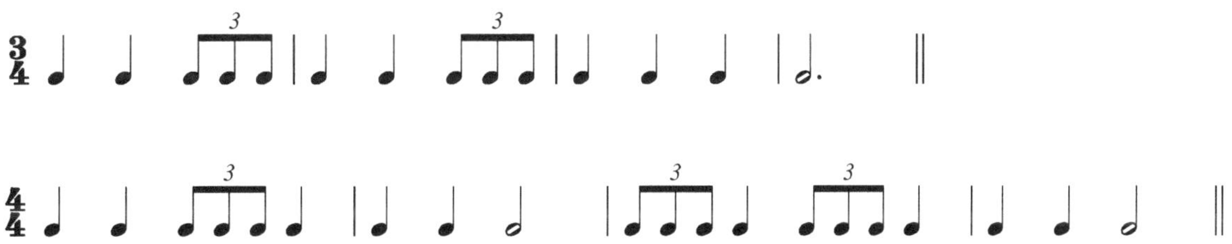

BONUS ACTIVITY

Say the examples above using rhythm sylables: | = ta, 𝅗𝅥 = ta-ah, 𝅗𝅥. = ta-ah-ah, ⌈3⌉ = triple-ti.

RESOURCES • 15

16

DOTTED RHYTHMS / TIES

Name ______________________________

DOTS ADD VALUE

Sometimes a note or rest has a **dot** after it, making that note/rest longer by half the value of the note itself. A **dotted rhythm** consists of a dotted note plus a shorter note, resulting in uneven rather than even rhythm.

Ex. A dotted half note is equal to a half note plus a quarter note.

A dotted quarter note is equal to a quarter note plus an eighth note.

All of these notes in simple meter can be followed by a dot and are named accordingly, with the dot always placed on the right side of the note:

= dotted whole note = 6 beats (4 + 2 = 6)

= dotted half note = 3 beats (2 +1 = 3)

= dotted quarter note = 1½ beats (1 + ½ = 1½)

= dotted eighth note = ¾ beat (½ + ¼ = ¾)

= dotted sixteenth note = ⅜ beat (¼ + ⅛ = ⅜)

These measures containing undotted patterns below have the same number of beats as the measures with dotted patterns directly underneath. First write the counts below each undotted and dotted pattern, then clap the undotted patterns, followed by the dotted patterns. Divide the class into two groups, having one group pat the undotted measures as the other half of the class claps the dotted patterns at the same time.

a.

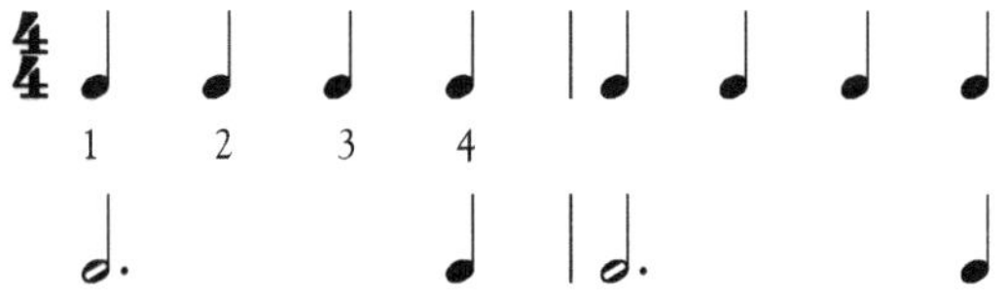

b.

c.

MATH AND DOTS

Remember that a dot after a note augments that note by adding half the value of the note. Fill in the number of beats given each of these dotted notes.

♩. =________ 𝅗𝅥. =________ ♪. =________ =________

Fill in these blanks.

If a 𝅗𝅥 = 2 beats, then a 𝅗𝅥. = __________ beats.

If a 𝅝 = 4 beats, then a = __________ beats.

If a ♩ = 1 beat, then a ♩. = __________ beats.

Using a line from the poem, "Talkin' Blues", first clap and say the line with no dotted notes (straight eighth notes), then repeat it, adding the dots to the notes as shown.

Ex.

DOTTED RESTS

A **dot** added to a **rest** also extends its duration by one-half, just like the corresponding notes, as shown by this chart.

Ex.

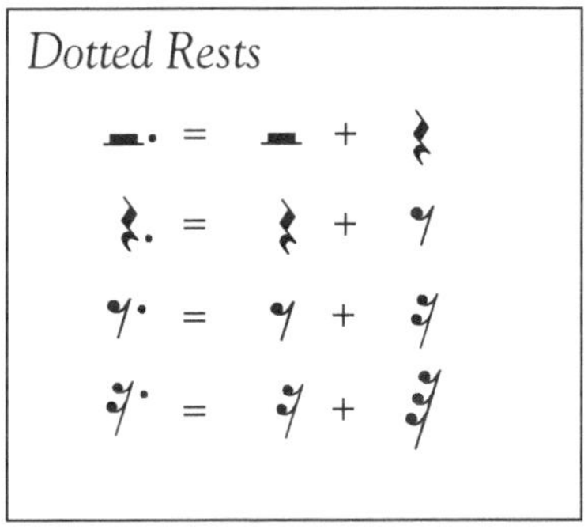

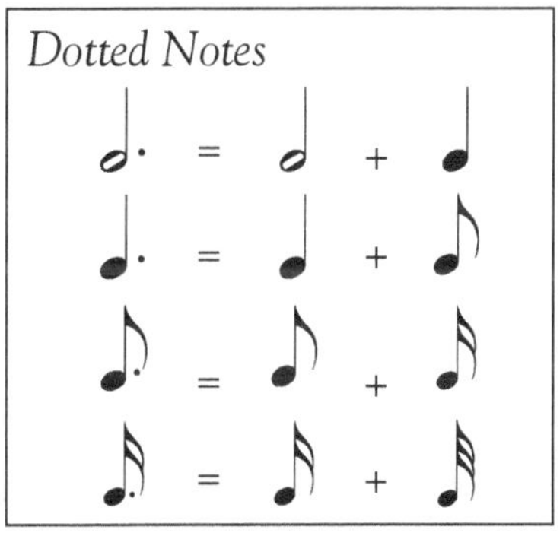

TIES

It is possible to join successive notes that are of the same pitch, by using a curved line to connect them, known as a **tie**. The first note is sounded, then held for the time duration of both the notes without the second note being sounded again. Notes of any value can be tied together as needed. The **tie** acts as a plus sign, extending the value of the first note.

Ex.

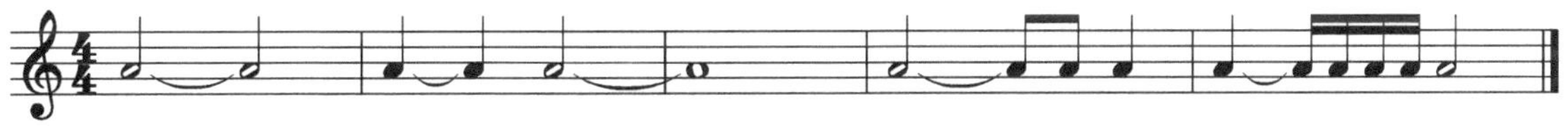

Clap and count these measures with tied notes.

ACCENTS / RHYTHM INSTRUMENTS

Name ______________________________

ACCENTS

Some beats are stronger than others and known as stressed or **accented** beats. Strong beats are usually heard at regular intervals, grouping the beats in twos (strong-weak), threes (strong-weak-weak) or fours (strong-weak-weak-weak) or even more.

An accented note, will usually catch the listener's attention more than the quiet beats. Longer notes in a rhythm pattern or phrase carry more weight and come on the strong beats, making it difficult to distinguish dynamics from the rhythm.

Every meter contains natural **accents**, counted this way:

2 = ONE two ONE two ONE two ONE two

3 = ONE two three ONE two three ONE two three

4 = ONE two *three four ONE two three four

6 = ONE two three *four five six ONE two three *four five six

*In 4 and slow 6 meters, there is often a **secondary** (less heavy) accent on a middle beat, in addition to the **primary** (heavy) accent on the first beat of each measure.

PRACTICE WITH ACCENTS

Clap the following lines, being louder on the underlined beats. In this way, the use of accents groups the beats together.

Number of Beats per Group													
	2	1	2	1	2	1	2	1	2	1	2	1	2
	3	1	2	3	1	2	3	1	2	3	1	2	3
	4	1	2	3	4	1	2	3	4	1	2	3	4

In the example below, circle the note that is on the strong beat.

RHYTHM INSTRUMENTS

Unpitched instruments are often referred to as 'rhythm' instruments and are played to strengthen inner rhythmic sense and enhance the music.

Experiment by using instruments to play the rhythm of the first beat of each measure (heavy timbre), the rhythm of the meter (steady beat) and the rhythm of the words (lighter timbre). Determine which instruments sound appropriate for each rhythm.

Through the use of percussion instruments in class, several concepts can be strengthened involving rhythm:

- keeping a steady beat
- varying tempo
- reading music notation
- determining musical form
- varying dynamics (strong and weak sounds)
- contrasting patterns

DISCOVER•PERFORM•CREATE

Discover which unpitched instruments can sustain a sound for several beats, then experiment playing in duple and triple meter. Students who are not playing can pat the steady beat as they wait their turn.

Perform the following parts for instruments as you sing the familiar song, "Yankee Doodle".

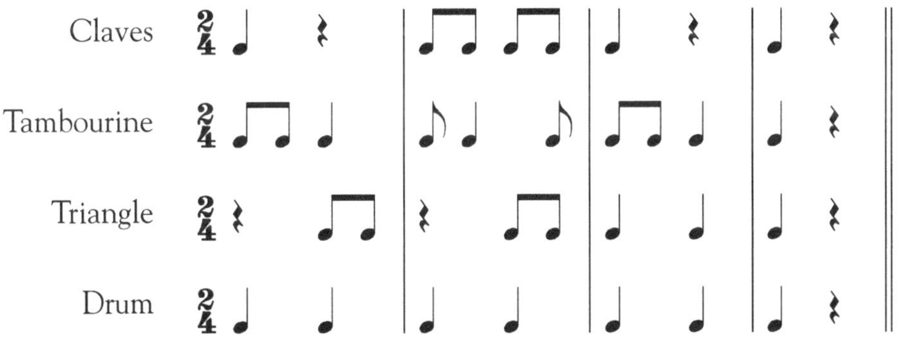

Divide into small groups and create your own percussion instrument parts for a familiar song. Perform your composition for the class as they sing.

BONUS QUESTION

Can you name the four families (groupings) of unpitched rhythm instruments?

SYNCOPATION

Name ______________________________

ACCENT THE OFF BEAT

In a rhythm pattern, when an accented note occurs on a usually weak beat, this is called **syncopation**. Normally, the first beat of a measure receives the greatest emphasis (accent), but composers sometime plan accents in unexpected places, such as 'off beats' or between beats. Syncopation also occurs when a note introduced on a weak beat is held over into a stronger beat. This technique is characteristic of jazz and ragtime music.

Ex. Steady Beat

Divided Beats

Tied Beats

Syn-co-pa

The most common example of syncopation is the rhythm of an eighth note on the downbeat followed by a quarter note, then followed by another eighth note. The pattern below shows a displacement of the normal accent, therefore accenting beats that would not normally be emphasized.

Ex. 

FOLLOW THE ACCENTS

The use of syncopation has appeared in European art music for centuries and is associated with dance rhythms from which modern jazz developed. Get accustomed to this emphasis by clapping and counting these examples.

Clap and count this pattern, stressing the strong beats.

Ex. 

Clap and count this pattern, stressing the weak half of the beats as marked.

Ex. 

Clap and count this example of tied beats with the stress markings.

Ex. 

Clap and say these examples, first with rhythm syllables (ta, ti and ta-ah), then clap and say them using the syllables under each example.

Ex. 1 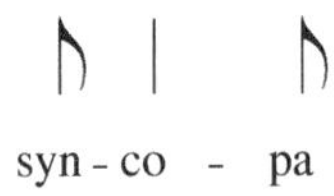

Ex. 2 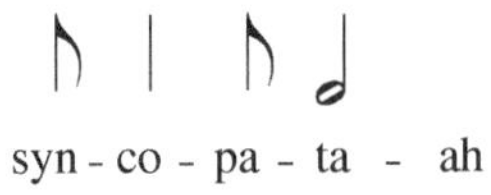

Ex. 3 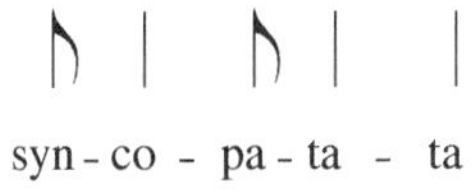

RECOGNIZING SYNCOPATION

Figure out the rhythm language for this line of the folk song, "Shoo, Fly, Don't Bother Me". Circle the syncopated rhythm, then clap the rhythm of the words.

In this Louisiana folk song below, "Mister Banjo", circle the measures that **do not** contain syncopation. As the class pats a steady beat, select a few students to play this song rhythm on unpitched instruments.

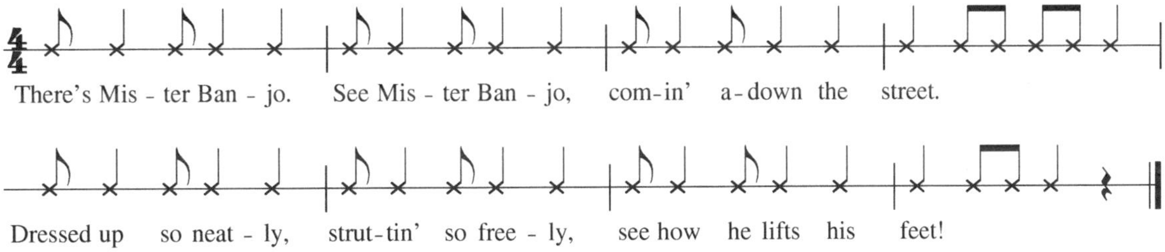

BONUS ACTIVITIES

1. Read the words of "Shoo, Fly, Don't Bother Me", substituting "syn-co-pa" for "shoo, fly, don't" in measures 1, 3 and 5.

2. Listen to a recording of "The Entertainer" by American composer, Scott Joplin, to hear examples of syncopation in ragtime music. Raise your hand every time you recognize a pattern of syncopation as you enjoy the music.

TEMPO / METRONOME

Name ______________________________

TEMPO = SPEED

The word **tempo**, an Italian term for 'time', is an indication of how fast the beat is moving and usually is referred to in terms of the number of beats per minute in music. The faster the beat, the faster the tempo, so a piece of music with an indicated tempo of sixty beats per minute will be slower than music with 100 beats per minute.

Composers usually indicate the tempo for a piece by placing specific Italian terms at the beginning. Even though few conductors and performers agree on a 'right' or exact tempo for a composition, these are some of the most frequently used terms to indicate the composer's preference. (slowest to fastest)

Slow tempo: *adagio, largo, lento*

Moderate tempo: *allegretto, andante, moderato*

Fast tempo: *allegro, presto, vivace*

Added to these words, the performer or conductor often finds a qualifying word such as *meno*, meaning 'less', *molto*, which means 'very' or 'much' and *non troppo*, meaning 'not too much'.

SLOW TO FAST

Fill in the blanks on the chart below with a word of your own that equals the Italian term in tempo markings, as they move from slow to fast.

Italian	English	Italian	English
1. *Largo*		6. *Allegretto*	
2. *Lento*		7. *Allegro*	
3. *Adagio*		8. *Vivace*	
4. *Andante*		9. *Presto*	
5. *Moderato*		10. *Prestissimo*	

Listen to recordings of several familiar pieces of music as you tap with the steady beat. Vary your selections from slow to fast examples.

METRONOME

Musicians use a mechanical or electrical device called a **metronome** to keep a steady beat or reproduce an exact tempo. Invented by J. N. Malzel in 1816, the early models consisted of a swinging rod or pendulum whose speed of movement could be varied by sliding a weight up or down the rod. The composer Ludwig Beethoven was one of the first musicians to use a metronome during his composing.

Most music moves at a metronome speed of between 60 and 160 beats per minute. For example, most marches move at MM (Malzel's metronome) 120 or 120 ticks per minute, each tick being the length of a quarter note.

Ex. *Largo* = 40 to 57 beats per minute

Adagio = 57 to 70

Andante = 71 to 89

Allegro = 90 to 135

Vivace = 136 to 170

Presto = 171 to 216

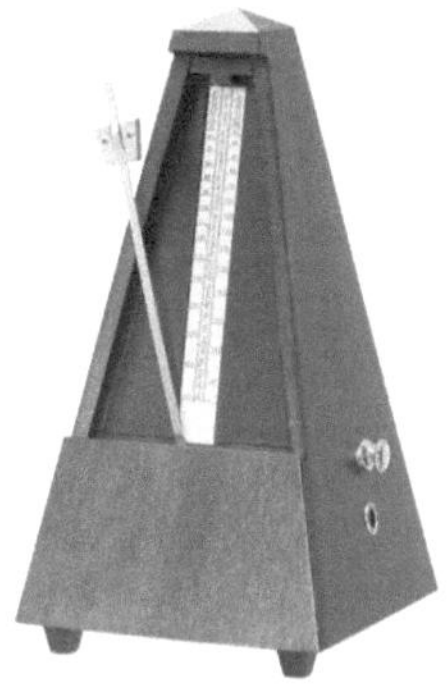

Modern metronomes have replaced the swinging pendulum with a clock or digital mechanism, but it is still widely used to indicate to the conductor or performer the suggested pace of a piece as set by the composer.

FOLLOW THE TEMPO

Rehearse the following rhythm patterns on unpitched instruments using the suggested metronome markings.

RESOURCES TEST 20

RHYTHM RECAP / TEST YOUR KNOWLEDGE

Name ____________________

In the last nine lessons, you have strengthened your understanding and use of rhythm in the areas of **meter**, **time signatures**, **dotted notes**, **rests**, **syncopation**, **tempo** and **accents**.

1. Give your own definition of these vocabulary terms.

   a. *Meter*____________________

   b. *Syncopation*____________________

   c. *Tempo*____________________

2. Match a time signature with the correct rhythm pattern by drawing a line from one to the other.

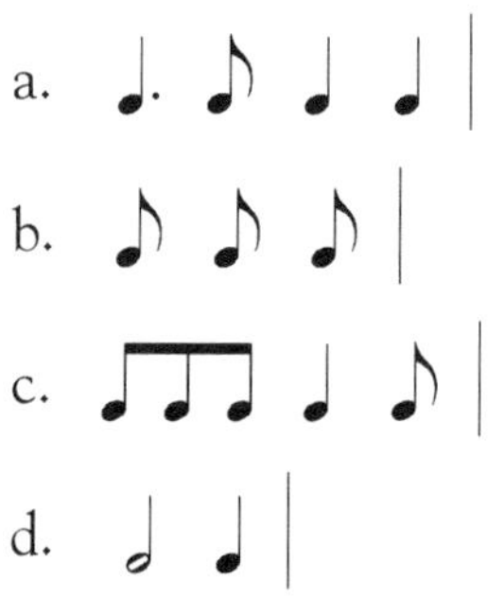

a. 6/8

b. 3/4

c. 4/4

d. 3/8

3. Give each of these examples a correct time signature.

4. Complete each measure by adding one rest of the correct value.

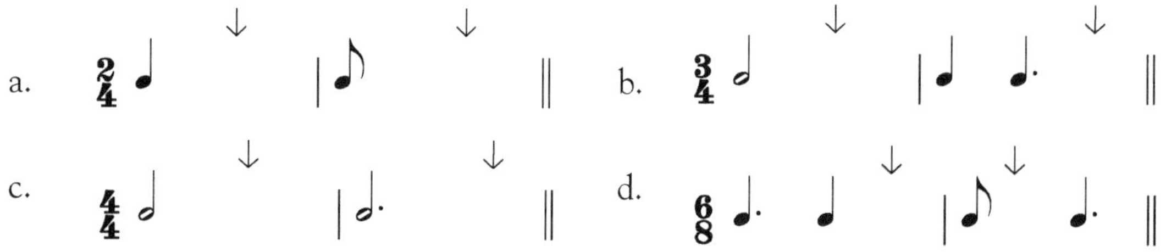

5. Fill in the blanks.

   a. Stressed beats are called __________and unstressed beats are called ________.

   b. A pattern of alternating strong and weak beats is called ____________ meter.

   c. Triple meter is comprised of alternating patterns of _____________, _______, _________beats.

   d. Compound meter is _______________meter with a top number in the time signature that is multiplied by the number _____________.

   e. Quadruple meter contains __________beats per measure.

6. Fill in the box with the correct number of notes or rests to equal one measure in each designated meter.

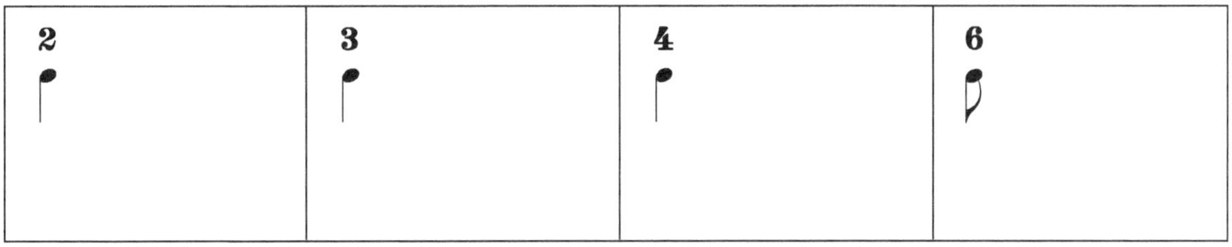

7. Circle the rhythm pattern that shows syncopation and put a rectangle around the compound meter.

8. Underline the strong beats and circle the triplet patterns in these examples.

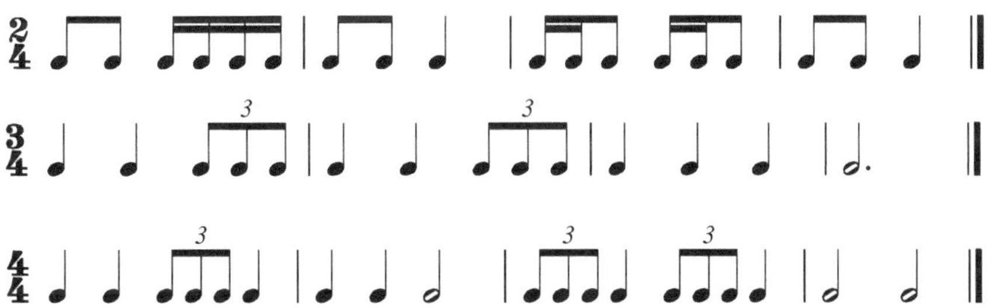

9. Give two examples of 'irregular' meter: _________________, _______________

10. Fill in the corresponding rest for each of these notes.

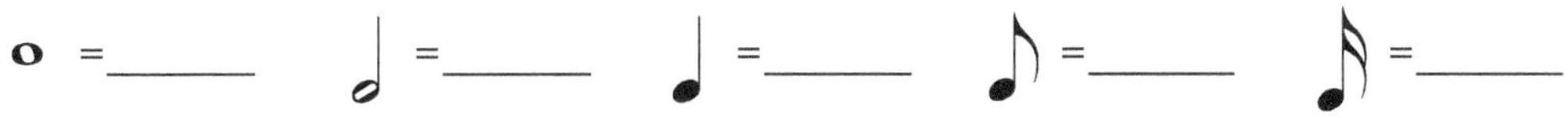

COUNTING NOTATION

Name ____

Musicians who learn to play an instrument, master the art of **counting** music notation to hone their skills. Often using a metronome (see Lesson 19) to set an accurate tempo, serious music students practice counting rhythm in preparation for playing musical exercises accurately. The process of "sight-reading" is strengthened by mastering the counting of rhythm patterns.

Necessary concepts that follow will help you put the pieces of **rhythm counting** into a meaningful sequence.

DIVIDED BEAT

Say the rhythm syllables for this example using **ta** (|), **ti ti** (⊓), and **ta-ah** (𝅗𝅥).

Ex.

Next, write the numbers for counting under the notes. For two eighth notes joined by a beam, say the count-number on the first note connected by the beam, then say the word 'and' on the second connected note. For half notes, clap the first beat, keeping hands clasped, pulsing outward on the second beat without clapping. Clap and count the example above aloud.

BEATS OF REST

When counting rhythm patterns that incorporate beats of rest, include the rests as part of the measure's total value. To show the position of the rest as you clap, put hand out, palms up, pulsing the silent beat in the air.

Ex.

Write in the counts under these examples, then clap and say the counts aloud, including the silent beats of rest.

TIED NOTES

Write the counts under this example including tied notes, then clap and count aloud. (Remember to not clap on tied notes.)

Ex.

DOTTED NOTES/SIXTEENTH NOTES

Remembering that dots following notes add half the value of the note, use the word 'and' to express the second half of a beat. In counting four sixteenth notes, joined by a beam, say '1 – e-& – a' (ah) to count all four notes on one beat.

Ex. 

Write the counts under this example, then clap it as you count aloud.

COMPOUND METER

With six beats in a measure and an eighth note receiving one count, a sixteenth note then receives ½ beat. With a faster tempo, $\frac{6}{8}$ meter feels as if it has two strong beats in each measure, with each beat divisible by three.

Ex. 

Write in the counts for this example, then clap it, counting aloud.

CUT TIME

If the bottom number of the time signature indicates that a half note receives one beat, equate this to the following example.

Ex. 

Write the counts in 'Cut Time', then clap it as you count aloud. Remember that another name for 'Cut Time' is 'Alle Breve'.

BONUS ACTIVITIES

1. Clap and count these examples.

a.  b. 

c.  d. 

2. Open your music textbook and find isolated measures of rhythm from a familiar song to clap and count.

BODY PERCUSSION

Name ______________________________

BODY PERCUSSION

Responding to rhythm is an integral part of learning to read music. Our bodies can produce rhythmical sounds to enhance musical performance and enjoyment when instruments are not available or another timbre is needed. These sounds are called **body percussion** and are categorized in four levels: **snapping, clapping, patting (patschen), and stamping**. Other unusual sounds are also often effective such as tongue clicking and chest thumping.

Practice and perform this example in $\frac{6}{8}$ meter, going from top to bottom, then in reverse. Next, divide the class into four equal groups and perform the example as a **rhythm canon** with each group getting one measure head start. Repeat the exercise several times in the process.

SPEECH PIECE WITH BODY PERCUSSION

Rhythm gets inside my head and won't let go!

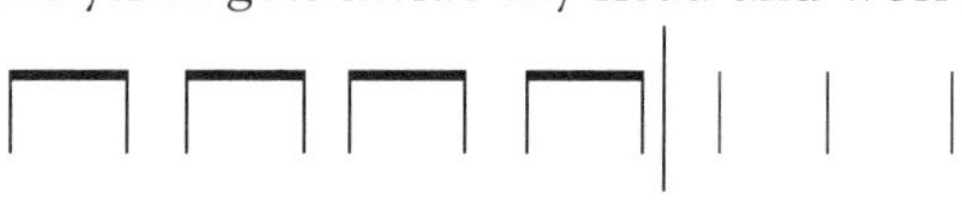

Even when I try to stop, it just says "no"!

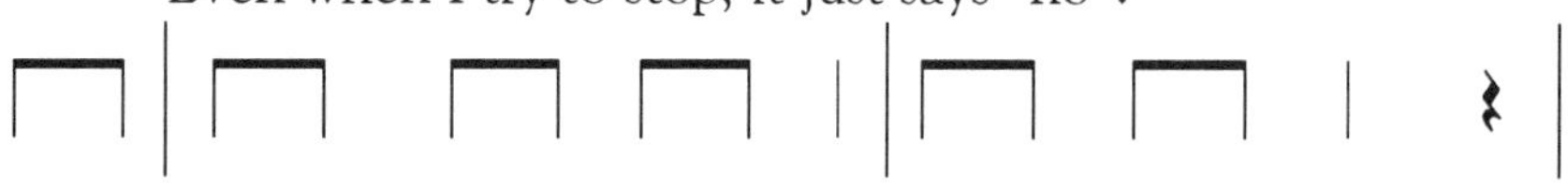

So I'm drumming with my fingers and tapping with my toes.

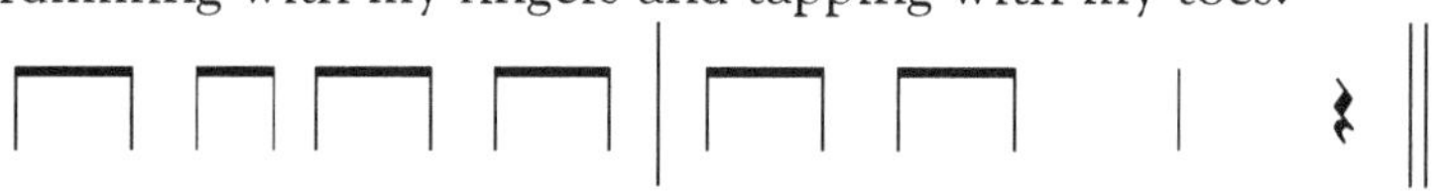

Rhythm is a part of me, but why? I just don't know!

Read the speech piece together from the previous page in $\frac{4}{4}$ meter, while patting a steady beat. Perform the poem using body percussion as suggested:

- clap all eighth notes
- pat all quarter notes
- snap all rests
- stamp the last words, "I just don't know!"

As the class repeats the poem with body percussion, have selected volunteers add an unpitched instrument as suggested:

- play a woodblock on eighth notes
- play a drum on quarter notes
- play finger cymbals on rests

CREATE A RONDO WITH BODY PERCUSSION

Using the **rondo** form of **ABACADA**, have the class decide upon a four-measure body percussion rhythm pattern to repeat as the A section. Write the class pattern on the board or transparency for reference, such as the one below:

Ex.

patsch clap clap patsch clap clap | clap snap snap patsch clap

stamp clap stamp clap | clap clap clap clap patsch snap

Divide the class into three small groups, one to create the **B** section, one to do the **C** section and another to make up a **D** section. These alternating sections may only be two measures in length. After these alternating patterns are composed and practiced several times, put the rondo together this way:

A	B	A	C	A	D	A
class	**group**	**class**	**group**	**class**	**group**	**class**

Repeat the rondo, using individual volunteers to perform the **B**, **C** and **D** sections in contrast to the class perform **A** section. Repeat several times with new volunteers.

BONUS ACTIVITY

Create rhythm patterns using body percussion to accompany one of your favorite songs, writing the patterns out for sharing with the class.

OSTINATO / MYSTERY TUNES

Name ______________________________

Pronounced (os-tee-NAH-to), an **ostinato** is a clearly defined melodic or rhythmic phrase which is repeated many times. Ostinato patterns can be strictly rhythmical using body percussion or can be phrases taken directly from the word-rhythm of a song. An ostinato can also be played on unpitched or melodic instruments, adding to the appeal of a song.

The term ostinato is derived from the word 'obstinate', which exactly describes how it is used. The plural version is **ostinati**, meaning more than one ostinato. Using a repetitive rhythm pattern aids concentration and promotes rhythmic confidence. An ostinato is often used as an accompaniment for a familiar song, possibly transferred to unpitched instruments after practice.

CREATING OSTINATI

Clap this simple ostinato repeatedly until it is secure, then clap it as you sing a favorite song in $\frac{4}{4}$ meter.

Ex. 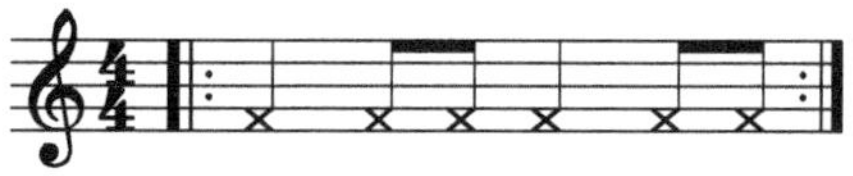

Betty Botter

Betty Botter bought some butter,
"But," she said, "the butter's bitter.
If I put it in my batter,
It will make my batter bitter,
But a bit of better butter
That will make my batter better."
So she bought a bit of butter,
Better than her bitter butter,
And she put it in her batter
And the batter was not bitter.
So 'twas better Betty Botter
Bought a bit of better butter.

Traditional Rhyme

Read the rhyme above as a class using a steady beat. Read it again tapping the rhythm of the words. What did you notice about the word rhythm? What would be the time signature?

Choose one line of the poem as an ostinato, having a small group say and tap that line repeatedly as the class reads the entire poem in rhythm.

Practice the following ostinati one at a time, then have a small group perform each one as the class reads the poem. As a finale, perform them all together with the poem.

- It's bitter, Betty Botter!

- You've got bitter butter.

- Bitter butter, better butter, bitter butter, better butter

Select volunteers to play these ostinato patterns on unpitched instruments, one at a time, then all together as the rhyme is spoken.

Choose a familiar song or poem and create your own two-measure rhythmic ostinato patterns to accompany them.

BONUS ACTIVITY: MYSTERY TUNES

See how many of these familiar songs you can identify by tapping the rhythm in each line below. Solving the mystery of a song's identity from the rhythm provided is proof you are putting several skills and concepts to use. After you know what each song is, create a rhythmic ostinato to accompany it as you sing.

1. 

Song Title:____

2. 

Song Title:____

3. 

Song Title:____

4. 

Song Title: ____

CONDUCTING / ANACRUSIS

Name ______________________________

Whether or not you will ever **conduct** a fine choir, band or orchestra, learning to be a **conductor** is a positive way to respond to rhythm. Information you have learned about **steady beat**, **accent** and **meter** will be useful as you practice this skill.

Shown below are standard conducting patterns used universally by conductors. In each pattern there is a strong downbeat followed by weaker upward pulses. The diagrams show the patterns for a right-handed director, but can be reversed for a left-handed person. Often, both hands are used for emphasis and sustaining one group of musicians as another group cuts off.

CONDUCTING PATTERNS

Practice each of these patterns slowly at first, then faster with appropriate recorded music and class singing.

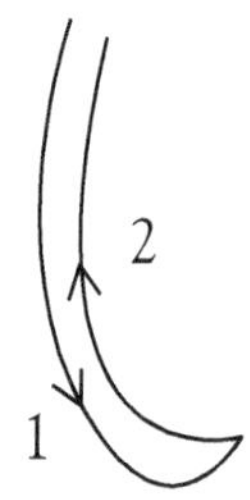

Two-Beat Pattern (down-up), counting 1-2

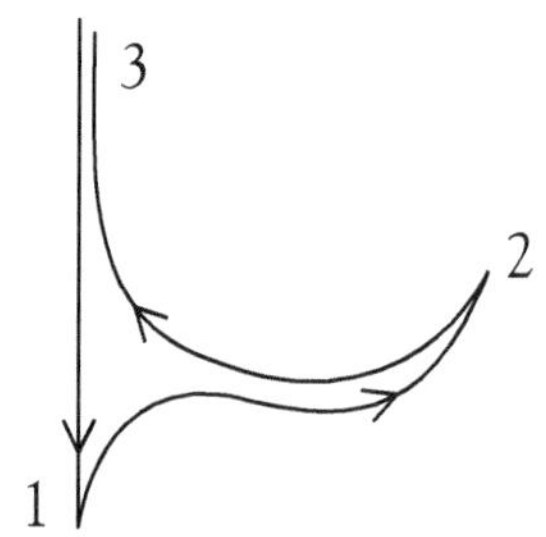

Three-Beat Pattern (down-right-up), counting 1-2-3

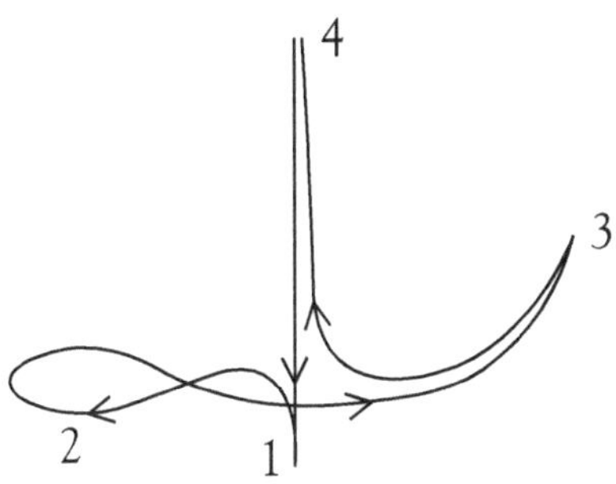

Four-Beat Pattern (down-left-right-up), counting 1,2,3,4

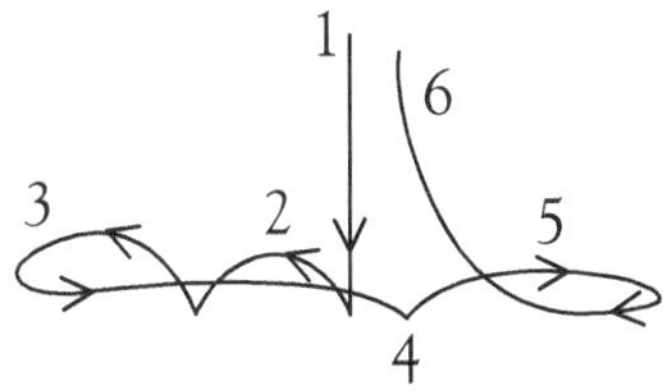

Six-Beat Pattern (down-left-left-right-right-up), counting 1,2,3,4,5,6

ANACRUSIS

Music does not always start on the first beat of the measure. You will notice that sometimes a piece starts one or more beats before the first strong downbeat. This beginning ahead of the downbeat is called an **anacrusis**, which is also referred to as a 'pick-up note'. An anacrusis consists of less than a full measure of counts, coming just before the first full measure of music.

When this happens, the last measure of the piece will supply the missing beats to constitute a full measure when added together.

Notice this beginning of "America, the Beautiful" to see how an 'anacrusis' is presented. See how many other songs you can find in your music textbook or octavo music featuring an 'anacrusis' at the beginning of a song.

Ex.

MATH / MUSIC

Name ______________________________

Rhythm and mathematics are synonymous, working together as sequential and precise sciences. Students could improve rhythmic skills by working math problems based on rhythm and note values. To solve the problems in this lesson, think of notes and rests as the addends and subtrahends, instead of numbers, then use your computation skills to work your way through the lesson.

ADD 'EM UP!

Put a numerical total value after adding the notes/rests in each of these examples in $\frac{4}{4}$ meter.

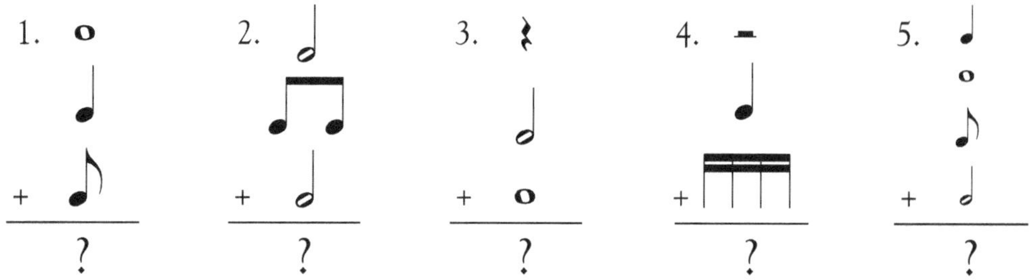

Put a numerical total value after adding the notes/rests in these examples with varied time signatures. When you have solved the problems, count aloud and clap each of the examples. (Remember: the bottom number of the Time Signature tells what type of note gets one beat.)

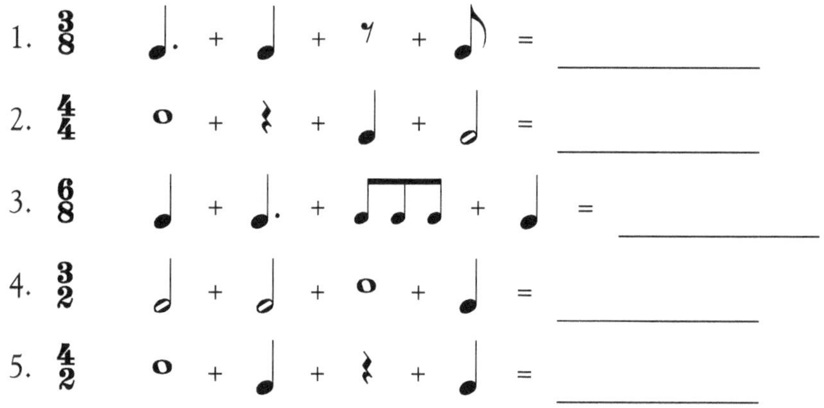

In each example below, supply one missing note or rest to equal the numerical total value provided. Check the time signature given for each problem.

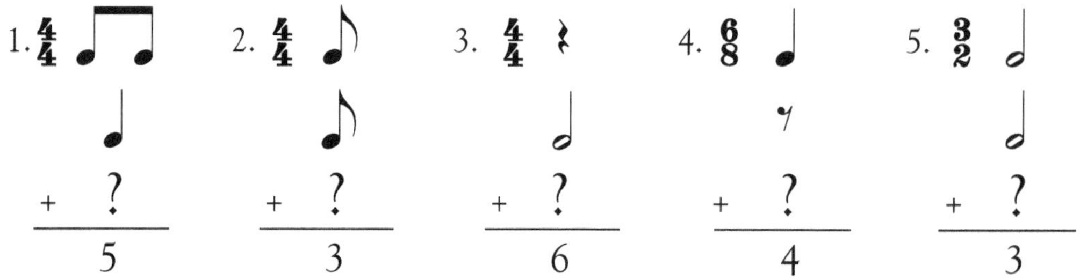

In $\frac{4}{4}$ time, provide one note in each example that would be subtracted from the first note shown in order to equal the answer given.

1. 𝅗𝅥 – ________ = ♪
2. 𝅗𝅥 – ________ = ♩
3. 𝅝 – ________ = 𝅗𝅥
4. 𝅝 – ________ = ♩
5. ♩ – ________ = ♪

Circle all the rhythm patterns below that equal ten beats in $\frac{4}{4}$ time.

1. 𝅗𝅥 𝅗𝅥 𝅗𝅥 𝅗𝅥 𝅗𝅥
2. 𝅝 𝄽 𝅗𝅥 ♩
3. ♪ 𝄾 ♩ 𝄽 𝅗𝅥 𝅗𝅥
4. ♫ 𝅝 𝄽 𝅗𝅥 ♩ ♩
5. 𝅝 𝅗𝅥 𝅝 𝅗𝅥

Provide a numerical total of beats for the rhythm syllables shown, in $\frac{4}{4}$ time.

1. ta ta ti-ti ta ta ta = ________
2. ta ti-ti ta ti-ti ta = ________
3. ta ti-ti ti-ti ta ta-a ta ta = ________
4. ti-ti ta-a ta ti-ti ta ta = ________
5. ta ta ti-ti ta ti-ti ta = ________

BONUS ACTIVITIES

1. Count aloud and clap the rhythm syllables in the five examples above.
2. Create a math problem involving notes and rests to share with the class.

REACTION • 24

26

IMPROVISATION

Name ______________________________

The process of **improvisation** enables you to be creative within a certain time frame, such as using eight beats or two measures. Based on developed rhythmic skills, you should be ready to create something original and interesting.

ECHO CLAP

Start with a familiar process called **echo clapping**. Have a leader (teacher) clap a four-beat pattern, echoed exactly by the class in strict rhythm. Alternate other volunteer students to be the next leaders, eventually switching to eight-beat patterns when ready. Here are some sample measures to get you started, or use samples from your flashcard sets (Lesson 11).

Ex. 

ORIGINAL ECHO

After several opportunities to echo-clap rhythm patterns exactly, have volunteers augment their responses to the leader's example by clapping an original pattern.

Ex.

Teacher

Student

RHYTHM CANON

Another step in building up to rhythmic improvisation is performing a **rhythm canon**. A leader (teacher) will clap a four-beat measure, then continue with new four-beat patterns without stopping. The class will clap the leader's first pattern as the leader begins the second measure as shown in this example and continue to echo the patterns without stopping, one measure behind the leader.

Ex.

Teacher:

Class:

Repeat this process choosing different, competent, volunteer students to take a turn as the new leader.

QUESTION AND ANSWER

To experience the process of phrase building, another rhythm response activity is called **question and answer**. The leader (teacher) will clap a rhythm pattern (question) lasting eight beats to which a student will answer with a different rhythm pattern. The leader's question should sound 'open-ended' followed by the student's answer that will sound 'final' and complete, as shown in this example:

Ex.

Teacher (Question):

Student (Answer):

GROUP/SOLO RONDO

Using the familiar rondo form - ABACADA (see Lesson 22), have the class:

- agree upon guidelines for establishing the **A** section as a group (i. e., how many measures, meter and which notes/rests will be used).
- create the **A** section, write it on the board or transparency, then practice clapping the pattern as a group.
- set guidelines for volunteers to improvise the alternating sections (i. e., how many measures and notes/rests to be used).
- select three volunteers who will improvise the alternating sections of the rondo without written notation.
- clap the rondo according to the sequence below, then vary the improvised sections by playing them on unpitched instruments.

A	B	A	C	A	D	A
group	solo	group	solo	group	solo	group

IMPROVISATION

Without any written notation, start with a one-measure $\frac{4}{4}$ meter pattern clapped by the leader (teacher) which the class will then echo. The leader next chooses a student who will clap a different improvised four-beat pattern, which is also echoed by the class. Have a student clap an original four-beat pattern immediately following the leader's new pattern. The class will echo both measures without a break in between. Set up several sequential eight-beat patterns, started by the leader and finished by a student for the class to echo.

BONUS ACTIVITY

1. After the leader (teacher) claps a four-beat pattern, layer the sound by having three or four students clap an improvised pattern simultaneously in response.
2. As a variation, play the improvised responses on unpitched instruments representing different timbre such as a woodblock, triangle and drum.

REACTION • 25

27

GAMES TO PLAY

Name ______________________________

Playing games with rhythmical themes gives your class an opportunity to have fun as you compete for team points, prizes or self esteem. The emphasis in this lesson will be on using what you have learned about rhythm to compete with members of your class.

Games played using rhythm could involve the kinds of notes, the reading of rhythm patterns and identifying familiar songs. The games suggested in this lesson start with an easier version, progressing to more advanced competition.

Create new variations of these games after you play both levels and are ready to reach a higher degree of thinking and achievement.

GAME ONE: "RHYTHM CONTAGION"

Have the class sit in a large circle, each with an unpitched instrument. Select a starter person who plays a four-beat rhythm pattern on the instrument. The next person to the right plays the first pattern followed by a different one of his own. The third person to the right must play the first pattern, the second pattern and then add an original. This sequence will continue until someone misses, then you start all over with a new starter.

Bonus Level: As the students become proficient at four-beat patterns, change to eight-beat patterns.

GAME TWO: "ROCK AND SOCK NAME GAME"

Have the class sit in a large circle, each with an unpitched instrument. Each student will play his or her first and last names in rhythm. As each name is played individually, the class will echo-play that name in reply. When every student has had a turn, have a volunteer play someone else's name (without looking at that person). When recognized, the person whose name was played will in turn play someone else's name and the game continues.

Bonus Level: Using a soft bean-bag or sock filled with newspaper, choose someone to be "it" and sit in the center of the circle. When a student plays someone else's name, "it" tosses the beanbag from the center of the circle at that person before they can pass the game on by playing a new person's name. When hit with the beanbag, that person becomes the new "it", and if the beanbag misses its mark, "it" must remain in the middle another time.

GAME THREE: "TRACE THE PATTERN"

Divide the class into four equal teams, sitting on the floor, one person behind another with each of the four leaders at the back of their team line. At the "ready-set-go" signal, the first team leader will tap out a four-beat rhythm pattern on the back of the person in front of her/him. The rhythm is then passed on up the line, tapped on each back in turn. When the rhythm gets to the first person in the line, that person claps the rhythm pattern he or she received. If the pattern is the same one that the leader started, that team gets a point.

Bonus Level: The teacher will hand the name of a familiar song written on a slip of paper to the team leader. At the appointed signal, the leader will tap out the word-rhythm of the first line of the song on the back of the student in front of him. The rhythm is then passed on from one student to the other, tapped on each back in turn. The first student at the front of the line who can identify the song, earns a point for their team.

GAME FOUR: "KEEP STANDING"

Divide the class into two equal groups with each group standing in lines on each side of the room. The leader (teacher) will hold up a familiar rhythm flashcard for the first person on Team A to read the rhythm and clap. If successful, the student goes to the end of the line to take another turn. If the pattern is missed, the student must sit down, out of the game. If the first person on Team A was successful, the first person on Team B gets a new rhythm. If Team A missed the rhythm, Team B tries to make the correction. The team with the most players standing at the end of the game wins, after everyone has had a turn.

Bonus Level: As a variation, have the leader clap four-beat patterns which the students take turns writing in notation on the board or on a transparency.

GAME FIVE: "IDENTIFY THE PATTERN"

Twelve examples of four-beat rhythm patterns are written on the board or transparency, numbered in order. Divided into two equal teams, each person gets a chance to clap one of the rhythms randomly, which a person on the other team must identify by number and re-clap for confirmation.

Bonus Level: When successful with four-beat patterns, advance to eight-beat patterns.

ADDED BONUS

After you have played these games, create a rhythmic game of your own for the class to play. Work in small "Cooperative Learning" groups with designated jobs for group members such as 'chairman' to lead the group, 'scribe' to write down the rules and sequence of the game, and 'scorekeeper.'

LISTENING MAPS

Name ______________________________

RHYTHM ROUNDELAY

As you begin this lesson, select a favorite, familiar piece of music with a moderate $\frac{4}{4}$ meter. Following the steps below, you will create an unusual rhythmic accompaniment for the music you have chosen.

1. Practice clapping each rhythm separately around the circle below, then perform the entire circle again without stopping.
2. Perform the circle repeatedly as you listen to your chosen song in $\frac{4}{4}$ meter.
3. Divide the class into two groups, then perform the circle as a round, having the second group begin one box (measure) after the first as marked.

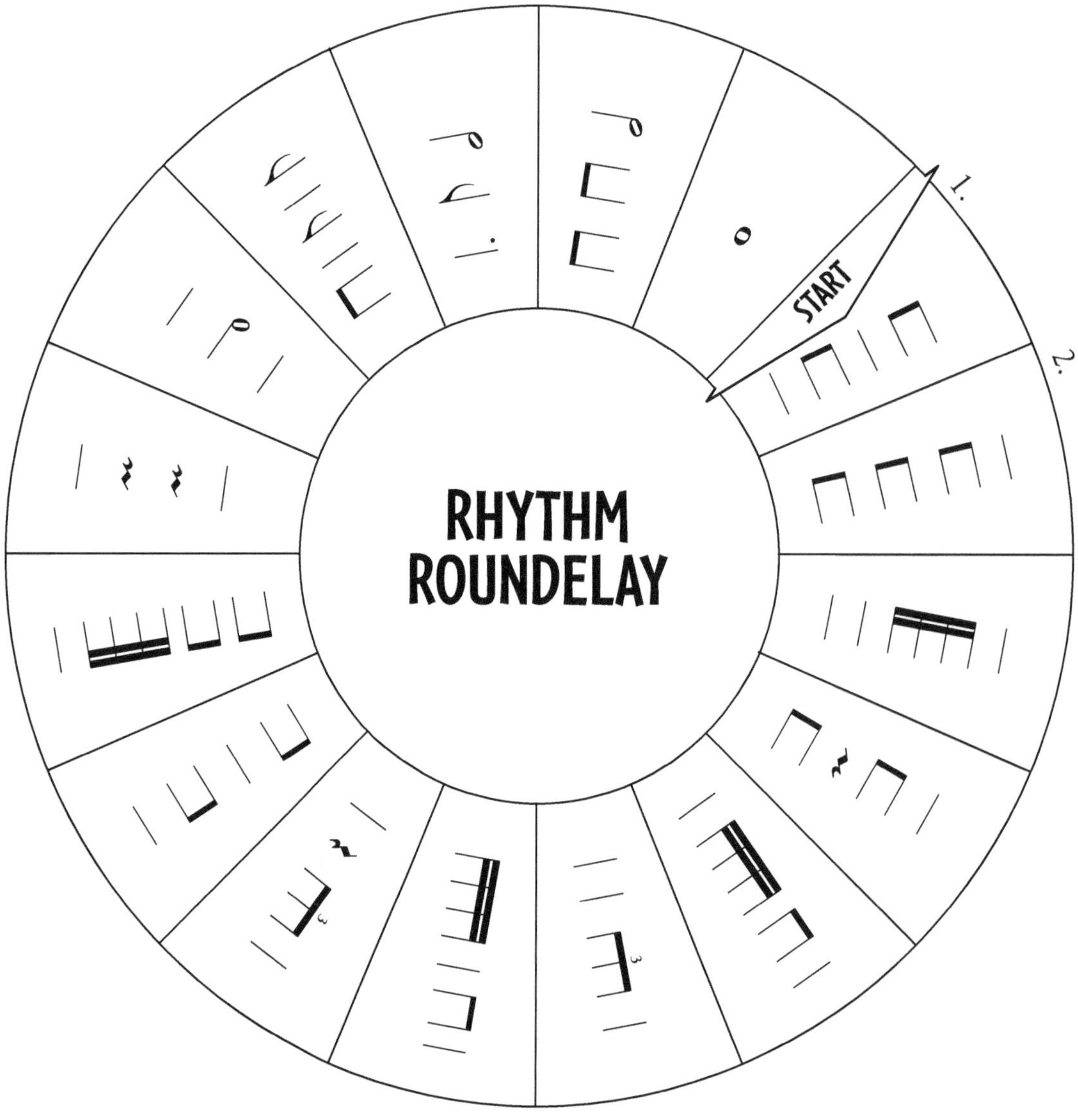

ADD DIFFERENT SOUNDS

4. Have the class create interesting vocal or body percussion sounds to represent each of the following icons:

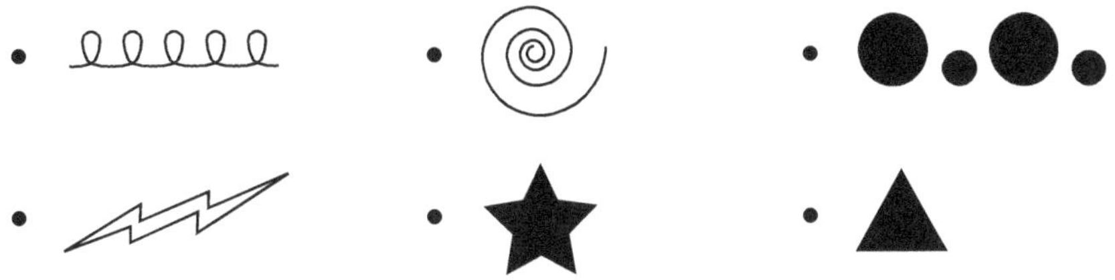

5. Practice each box of the circle below, using these sounds, giving each box four beats. Next, perform the whole circle without stopping.
6. Divide the class into two groups, then perform the circle as a round, having the second group start one box after the first as marked.

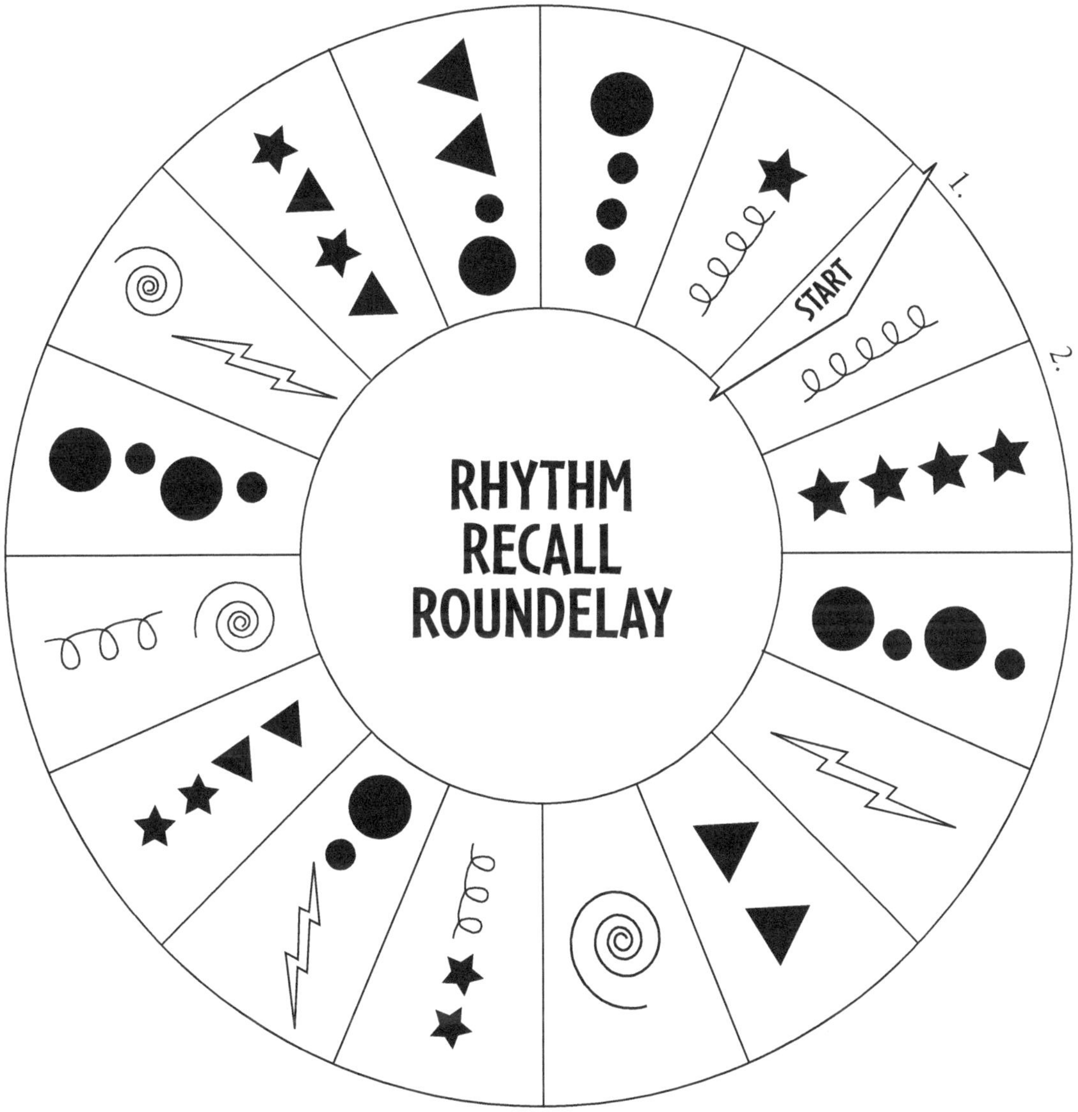

BONUS ACTIVITY

Perform both circles simultaneously in two groups, then in four groups as a round.

REACTION • 27

29

COMPOSITION

Name ______________________________

BE A COMPOSER

Try your skills at becoming a rhythmic composer by completing the following activities using information you have gained throughout the lessons in this book.

- Create eight measures of rhythm patterns below, making each measure different from the others.

$\frac{2}{4}$ __ __ | __ __ | __ __ | __ __ | __ __ | __ __ | __ __ | __ __ |

- Clap, pat or play your composition above on unpitched instruments as you listen to a famous march.

- Compose a rhythm piece below in ABA form, making the 'A' sections identical with a contrasting 'B' section.

$\frac{3}{4}$ A ______ | ______ | ______ | ______ |

B ______ | ______ | ______ | ______ |

A ______ | ______ | ______ | ______ |

- Count aloud and clap your composition as you listen to a waltz, minuet or jazz-waltz, then share it with the class.

CREATE AN ACCOMPANIMENT

On the next page you will create a rhythmic accompaniment for the traditional folk song, "Mama Don't 'Low".

Fill the boxes above the printed music with appropriate rhythm patterns to enhance this lively song, repeating some patterns as desired. Perform your composition by clapping each rhythm, then play the rhythms on unpitched instruments including a washboard, musical bones or spoons. Have half the class sing the song as others play the rhythms shared by the class.

MAMA DON'T 'LOW

Traditional

REACTION • TEST 30

PUTTING IT ALL TOGETHER

Name ________________________________

Choose the best answer for each of the following questions.

____1. Rhythm is
a. a melody
b. the steady beat
c. a harmony part
d. note groupings

____2. An accent refers to
a. rondo form
b. strong beats
c. weak beats
d. duration

____3. Another term for 'cut time' is
a. fermata
b. pulse
c. alle breve
d. steady beat

____4. A bar line is
a. horizontal
b. vertical
c. syncopated
d. curved

____5. A steady beat is
a. consistent
b. syncopated
c. horizontal
d. vertical

____6. Rondo form is
a. AAB
b. ABC
c. ABA
d. ABACADA

____7. The syllable "ta" refers to
a. two sounds per beat
b. one sound per beat
c. a rest
d. a measure

____8. The syllables "ti ti" refer to
a. two sounds per beat
b. one sound per beat
c. a rest
d. a measure

____9. Attached to a notehead is
a. a flag
b. a stem
c. a fermata
d. a tie

____10. A quarter note gets
a. three beats
b. two beats
c. one beat
d. no beat

____11. A half note
a. is colored in
b. has a flag
c. gets two beats
d. has no stem

____12. Joining two eighth notes is
a. a flag
b. a bracket
c. a stem
d. a beam

____13. A whole note
a. is colored in
b. has no stem
c. gets two beats
d. gets one beat

____14. On a staff, a half rest sits
a. on the 3rd line
b. on the 2nd line
c. on the 1st line
d. on the 5th line

____15. Two half notes equal
a. a whole note
b. a quarter note
c. an eighth note
d. a triplet

____16. Four quarter notes equal
a. 2 eighth notes
b. 4 eighth notes
c. 2 half notes
d. 2 whole notes

____17. On a staff, a whole rest hangs from
a. the 2nd line
b. the 4th line
c. the 5th line
d. the 3rd line

____18. A bar line
a. joins notes
b. means repeat
c. sets measures
d. ends a song

____19. A double bar line means
a. the end
b. repeat
c. go faster
d. hold

____20. A quarter rest
a. lasts 4 beats
b. lasts 2 beats
c. lasts 1 beat
d. is dotted

____21. In each measure, duple meter has
a. two beats
b. four beats
c. three beats
d. six beats

____22. Music with three beats in each measure is
a. common time
b. duple meter
c. cut time
d. triple meter

____23. In $\frac{6}{8}$ meter, a dotted quarter note
a. gets 1 beat
b. gets 2 beats
c. gets 3 beats
d. gets 4 beats

____24. In $\frac{6}{8}$ meter, a dotted half note gets
a. two beats
b. three beats
c. four beats
d. six beats

____25. "Row, Row, Row Your Boat" is in

a. $\frac{3}{8}$ time c. $\frac{3}{4}$ time
b. $\frac{6}{8}$ time d. $\frac{4}{4}$ time

____26. An example of complex meter is

a. $\frac{3}{4}$ time c. $\frac{7}{8}$ time
b. $\frac{6}{8}$ time d. $\frac{4}{4}$ time

____27. Quintuple meter is

a. $\frac{5}{4}$ time c. $\frac{2}{4}$ time
b. $\frac{4}{4}$ time d. $\frac{6}{8}$ time

____28. Music with no steady beat is called

a. non metric c. duple
b. compound d. triple

____29. A triplet is

a. 2 sounds per beat c. no sound
b. 3 sounds per beat d. 4 sounds

____30. A time signature is found

a. at the song's end c. after sharps
b. in each measure d. over flats

____31. Common time is

a. $\frac{2}{4}$ time c. $\frac{4}{4}$ time
b. $\frac{3}{4}$ time d. $\frac{6}{8}$ time

____32. A rhythm instrument that can sustain a long sound is

a. a drum c. claves
b. a woodblock d. a triangle

____33. Syncopation puts accents on

a. repeated notes c. steady beats
b. rests d. weak beats

____34. A tempo marked 'largo' would be

a. loud c. choppy
b. slow d. fast

____35. A metronome is

a. a drum stick c. a CD player
b. a recorder d. a beat device

____36. A form of body percussion is

a. moving c. jumping
b. clapping d. sliding

____37. An ostinato is

a. a repeated pattern c. an opera song
b. a soft pattern d. a cymbal

____38. An anacrusis is

a. a pick-up note c. accented
b. the downbeat d. a steady beat

____39. If two notes of the same pitch are connected by a curved line, it is

a. an anacrusis c. a tie
b. an accent d. a retardando

____40. A double bar with two dots means

a. to go faster c. end the piece
b. to repeat d. change tempo

____41. Beats of measured silence are

a. accents c. dots
b. signatures d. rests

____42. If a dot after a note adds half the value of a note, a dotted half note

a. gets 3 beats c. gets 5 beats
b. gets 1½ beats d. gets 2½ beats

____43. A letter 'C' with a line through it means

a. to count c. to connect
b. cut time d. to accent

____44. A note with two flags is

a. an 8th note c. a 32nd note
b. a 16th note d. a whole note

____45. A hemiola has

a. five beats c. six beats
b. seven beats d. eight beats

____46. In $\frac{3}{2}$ time, a half note gets

a. one beat c. three beats
b. two beats d. four beats

____47. Another word for duration is

a. value c. dynamics
b. steady d. ostinato

____48. The first beat of a measure is

a. the tempo c. the pulse
b. the downbeat d. syncopated

____49. The rhythm syllables for 'United States' would be

a.  c. 
b.  d. 

50. Cross-rhythms are often found in

a. Austria c. Australia
b. Africa d. Alabama

ANSWERS

SECTION 1: RHYTHM READINESS

Page 2:
(Recognizing Rhythm – underline strong beats in "Thirty Days")
<u>Thir</u>ty <u>days</u> <u>has</u> Sep<u>tem</u>ber,
<u>A</u>pril, <u>June</u> <u>and</u> No<u>vem</u>ber.
<u>All</u> our <u>days</u> are <u>filled</u> with <u>rhy</u>thm,
<u>Head</u> to <u>toe</u> and <u>in</u>side <u>out</u>.
<u>Days</u> of <u>rhy</u>thm, <u>beat</u> and <u>won</u>der
<u>Make</u> me <u>want</u> to <u>dance</u> and <u>shout</u>!

Page 3:
(Bonus Questions)
1. George Gershwin
2. beat, pulse, tempo and accents

Page 5:
(Matching)
1. f 2. j 3. d 4. a 5. g 6. h 7. i 8. c 9. b 10. e

(Scrambled Terms)
1. DURATION 2. FERMATA 3. METRONOME
4. OSTINATO 5. SYNCOPATION

(Fill in the Blanks)
1. downbeat 2. half the value 3. cut time 4. pulse
5. divide the staff into measures

(Bonus Activity)
1. An anacrusis is a pick-up note which comes before a downbeat.
2. A hemiola is a six-beat measure with beats divided into 2 groups of 3 or 3 groups of 2 beats.

Section 2: RHYTHM RELEVANCE

Page 7:
(Bonus Questions)
1. number 5 because of five players at once
2. numbers 3 and 7 because of only two players
3. numbers 1, 4, and 8 because of four players
4. yes, non-metric
5. beat and pulse

Page 11:
Emily Brown – ⊓ | | Z
Teddy McPherson – | ⊓ | |
Dulciana York – ⊓ ⊓ | Z
Bob Jones – 𝅗𝅥 𝅗𝅥
Amber Williams – | | | |

(Matching)
1. c 2. a 3. e 4. b 5. d

(Bonus Question)
AB

Page 13:
(Bonus Questions)
1. 32nd note 2. two beams 3. whole, half, and quarter notes

Page 14:

16th	8th	half	whole	quarter
¼ beat	½ beat	2 beats	4 beats	1 beat

Page 15:
(True/False)
1. T 2. F 3. F 4. T 5. T

(Bonus Questions)
1. 48 sixteenth notes
2. 26 beats

Page 16:
(Match Them Up)
1. e 2. d 3. b 4. a 5. c

Page 17:
(Music and Math Team Up)
1. 𝅗𝅥 2. 𝄽 3. 𝄼 4. 𝄽 5. 𝄽 6. 𝅝

(Bonus Questions)
1. Yes, a 32nd rest, 1/8 beat 2. 9 beats

Page 18:

1. 

2. 

3. 

Page 19:

1. 

2. 

3. 

(Bonus Question)

Page 20:
1. (definitions in own words)
   a. Duration is the length of time given to specific notes and/or rests.
   b. An accent is emphasis or stress on a musical tone, beat or chord.

2. 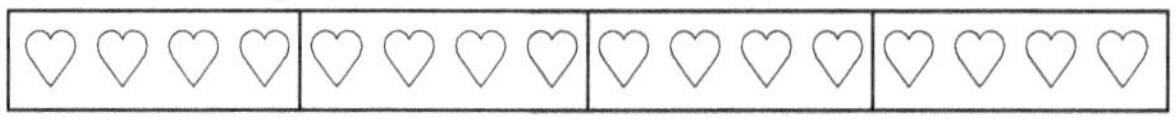

3. 

5. 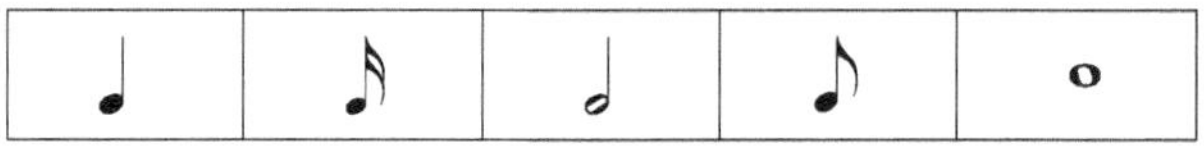

Page 21:
6. notehead, stem and flag
7. (8.)

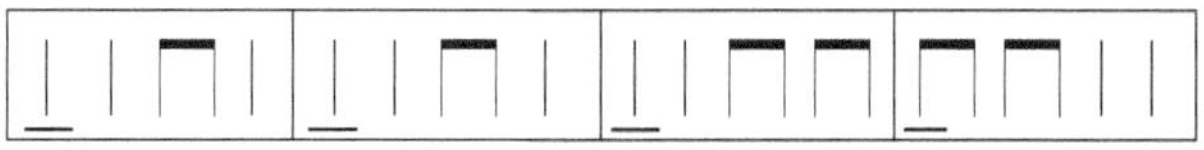

9. (Fill in the Blanks)

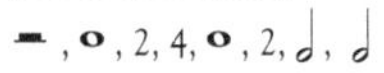

10. (True or False)
a. F b. F c. T d. F e. T f. F g. T h. T

11. a. 3 b. 4 c. 4 d. 4

Section 3: RHYTHM RESOURCES

Page 24:
6 = six beats to a measure
8 = an eighth note gets one beat
3 = three beats to a measure
4 = a quarter note gets one beat
3 = three beats to a measure
2 = a half note gets one beat

Page 25: (Time Signatures)
a. 2/4
b. 6/8
c. 3/4
d. 4/4
e. 6/8 or 3/4

Page 27:
1. Duple (strong – weak) Triple (strong – weak- weak)
2. 1st and 3rd (strong) 2nd and 4th (weak) 1st (strongest)
3. triple
4. S W W S W W S W W S W W

Page 28: (Chart)

TIME SIGNATURE	6/8	6/4	9/16	9/8	12/8	12/4
BEATS PER MEASURE	2	2	3	3	4	4
BASIC BEAT NOTE	♩.	𝅗𝅥.	♪	♩.	♩.	𝅗𝅥.

Page 29:
(Underline Strong Beats)
(Rhythm Syllables)

Page 31:
(Circle the Triplets)

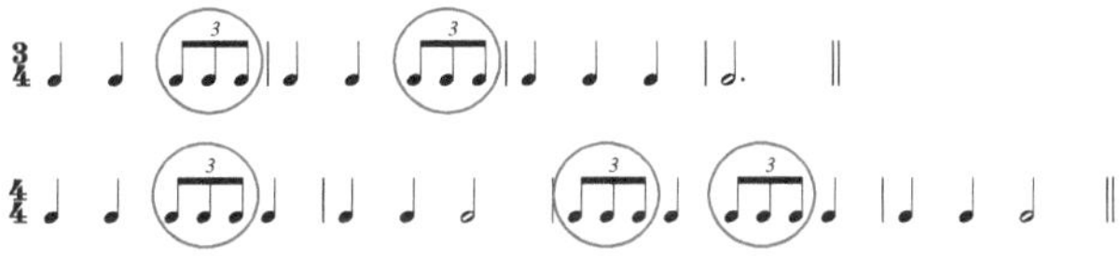

Page 32:
(Write the Counts)

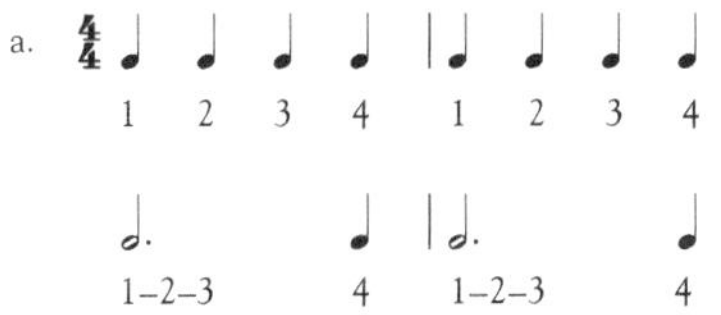

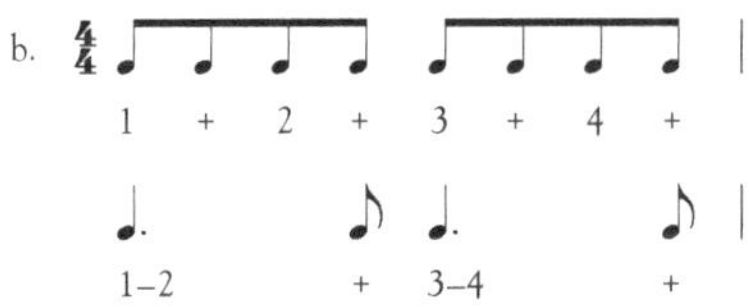

Page 33:
(Number of Beats)

♩. = 1½ 𝅗𝅥. = 3 𝅘𝅥𝅯 = ¼ o. = 6

(Fill in the Blanks)
3, 6, 1½

Page 34:
(Circle the Strong Beat)

Page 35:
(Bonus Question)
Woods, metals, shakers/scrapers and drums

Page 37:
(Circle the Syncopated Rhythm)

(Circle the Measures with no Syncopation)

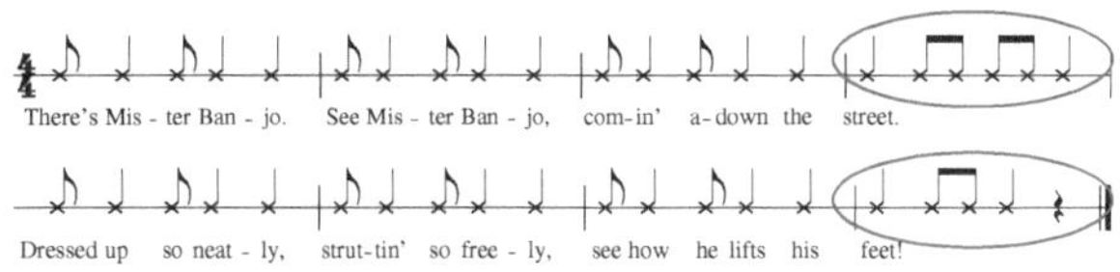

Page 40: (Definitions in own words)

1. a. Meter is the regular pattern of beats in music.
   b. Syncopation is the placing of strong accents on usually weak beats.
   c. Tempo is the pace at which a piece of music is performed.
2. (Matching)

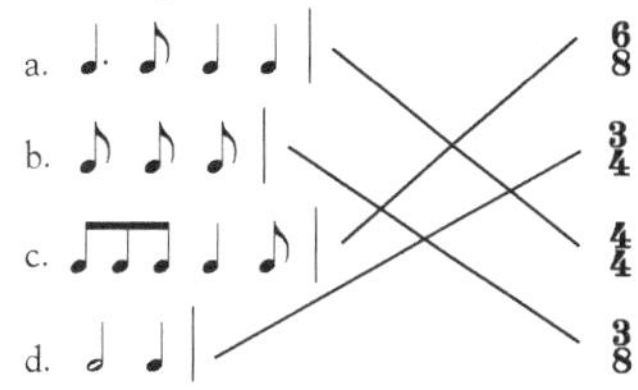

3. 4/4, 3/4, 5/4
4. (Complete each Measure)

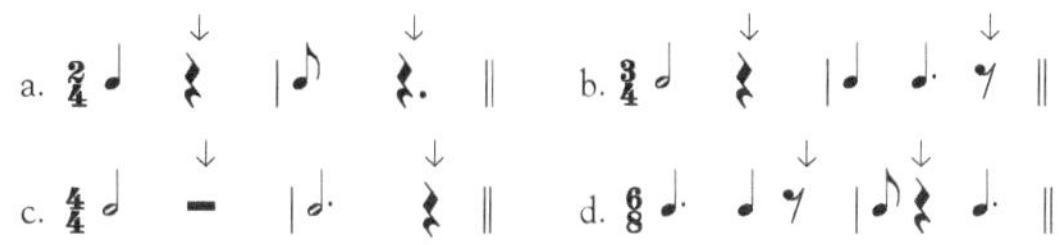

Page 41:
5. (Fill in the Blanks)
a. strong, weak b. duple c. strong, weak weak d. simple, three e. four

7. (Circle/Rectangle)

8. (Underline/Circle)

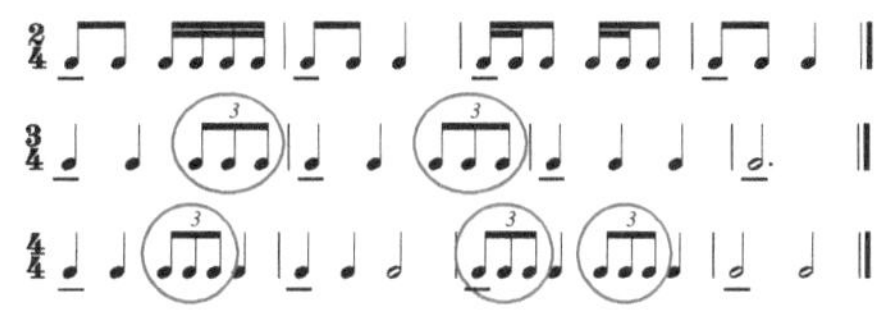

9. (Irregular Meter) 5/8 and 7/8
10. (Draw Rests)

Section 4: RHYTHM REACTION

Page 42:
(Divided Beat)

1–2 1 2 1–2 1–2 1 2 1 & 2 & 1–2

(Beats of Rest)

1-2-3-4 1-2 3-4 1 2 3 4 1-2 3 4

1-2 3 4 1-2-3-4 1 2-3 4 1-2 3-4 1-2-3-4

(Tied Notes)

1 2 3&4& 1 2 3&4& 1-2 3&4 1-2 3&4

Page 43:
(Dotted and Sixteenth Notes)

1 2&3-4 1-2&3-4 1e&a 2&3-4& 1&2-3 4 &

(Compound Meter)

1 2 3 4-5-6 1 2 &3 4-5-6 1-2 &3 4-5 6

(Cut Time)

1 2 1 & 2 1 & 2 & 1 e & a 2 & 1-2

(Bonus Activities)

1 2 & 3 e&a 4 1 2 & a 3 & 4

1-2 3 4 5 6 1 2-3 & 4-5-6 1 2 3&4 5 6& 1 2 3 4-5-6

Page 46:
The word rhythm of "Betty Botter" is made of only eighth notes.
The time signature would be $\frac{4}{4}$.

Page 47:
(Song Titles)
1. "Jingle Bells"
2. "The Star-Spangled Banner"
3. "America, the Beautiful"
4. "Over the River and Through the Woods"

Page 50:
(Numerical Value)
1. 5½ 2. 5 3. 7 4. 4 5. 7½

(Numerical Value, Notes/Rests)
1. 7 2. 8 3. 10 4. 4½ 5. 3½

(Supply the Note/Rest)

Page 51:
(Note Subtracted)

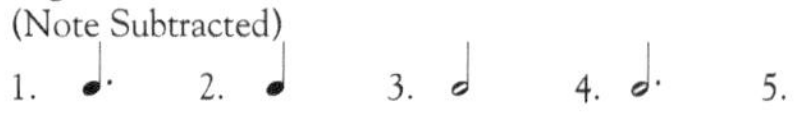

(Circle Ten Beats)

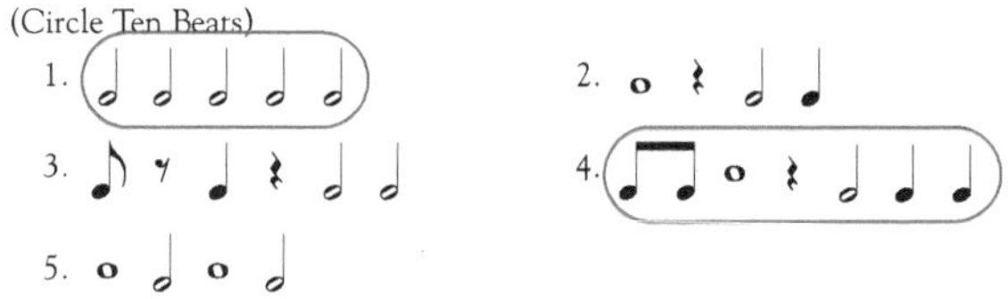

(Rhythm Syllables)
1. 6 2. 5 3. 8 4. 7 5. 6

Page 60 - 61:
(Putting It All Together)

1. d	2. b	3. c	4. b	5. a
6. d	7. b	8. a	9. b	10. c
11. c	12. d	13. b	14. a	15. a
16. c	17. b	18. c	19. a	20.c
21. a	22. d	23. c	24. d	25. b
26. c	27. a	28. a	29. b	30. c
31. c	32. d	33. d	34. b	35. d
36. b	37. a	38. a	39. c	40. b
41. d	42. a	43. b	44. b	45. c
46. a	47. a	48. b	49. c	50. b

ABOUT THE AUTHOR

Betsy Henderson is the Fine Arts Coordinator for Garland ISD, Garland, Texas, where she directs the award-winning Garland All-City Girls Choir. With degrees from Midwestern State University and the University of North Texas, she has served as elementary state chairmen for both the Texas Music Educators Association and the Texas Choral Directors Association. An author of the music textbook series, *Share the Music*, published by Macmillan/McGraw-Hill Company, Betsy has also written *The Composers Special Guide*, published by Hal Leonard.